Prompt Engineering Mastery: How to Optimize Interactions with Large Language Models

Authored by

Sumit Tripathi
Department of Big Data Analytics
Goa Institute of Management
Goa, India

Prompt Engineering Mastery: How to Optimize Interactions with Large Language Models

Author: Sumit Tripathi

ISBN (Online): 979-8-89881-360-4

ISBN (Print): 979-8-89881-361-1

ISBN (Paperback): 979-8-89881-362-8

Published by Bentham Science Publishers Pte. Ltd. Singapore,

in collaboration with Eureka Conferences, USA.

First published in 2026.

Bentham Science Publishers Pte. Ltd.
No. 9 Raffles Place
Office No. 26-01
Singapore 048619
Singapore
Email: subscriptions@benthamscience.net

BENTHAM SCIENCE

CONTENTS

PREFACE

Artificial intelligence (AI) has transformed how people interact with technology. One of its most significant accomplishments has been the ability to connect with machines using natural language, bringing AI's future closer to reality. This transformation is at the heart of Large Language Models (LLMs), which have emerged as extremely effective tools for understanding, producing, and participating in human-like communication. However, the promise is not fully realized without a specific skill: so-called rapid engineering. In essence, prompt engineering is the process of defining the inputs that a language model uses to generate an output. Now that LLMs are truly taking off and maturing, this technique of designing prompts is critical in realizing their full potential. So, Prompt Engineering Mastery: How to Optimize Interactions with Large Language Models aims to provide comprehensive assistance on understanding and mastering the principles that define an effective prompt. This book would be an excellent resource for anyone interested in developing LLMs to their full potential in their areas of expertise.

This book explores the link between prompt and response, demonstrating how slight adjustments to the prompt's form and language can significantly impact the quality of the outcome. It discusses LLM architecture, text tokenization, and strategies such as few-shot learning and iterative refinement, which are used in practice to achieve more sophisticated and accurate results. Each volume builds on the previous one, providing the information required to work with LLMs at the highest level. It goes into detail about real-world applications such as content development and marketing, customer assistance, education, and legal paperwork. This provides insights into how the specificity of prompts will make AI-generated content more efficient and relevant. Ethical concerns, such as bias and accountability, are addressed to ensure the appropriate use of AI technologies.

This book provides a thorough understanding of the underlying ideas that make LLMs so effective, as well as practical tools and approaches for accelerating engineering. As AI evolves, those who master prompt engineering will be well positioned to lead in this rapidly changing field. The capacity to properly prompt LLMs will open up new options in a variety of fields, including improved creative writing, automated customer service, and enhanced data analysis. Exploring the contents of this book is likely to be advantageous for a better understanding of rapid engineering and its future role in AI communication, as well as for empowering individuals to work more successfully with Large Language Models to produce amazing results.

Sumit Tripathi
Department of Big Data Analytics
Goa Institute of Management
Goa, India

CHAPTER 1

The Basics of AI Language Models: Introduction and Principles of Prompting

Abstract: The chapter describes the principles of AI language models, as well as the art and science of prompting, which, in turn, helps people talk to AI systems efficiently. It highlights the importance of AI systems such as GPT-3, GPT-4, and Gemini, as well as the essence of their impact in natural language processing (NLP). These methods changed communication between humans and machines, where the AI system could understand, process, and create human language. An essential aspect of this interaction is *"prompting."* The AI's final answer relies heavily on the human side inputting the right and contextually clear instructions. The chapter details the effects of well-structured prompts and output in the form of tips on how to change and modify prompts for competent results. Additionally, it covers other uses of AI models in content production, customer support, teaching, and even legal documents, marking the opportunity for innovation and efficiency. The future of AI language models is also presented in terms of ethical issues, bias, and changes in these systems' capabilities regarding text generation.

Keywords: AI language models, Contextual prompting, Ethical AI, Machine learning, Natural Language Processing (NLP), Prompt engineering.

INTRODUCTION

The last few years have seen some of the most fundamental advancements in artificial intelligence (AI) — and natural language processing (NLP) is one of the fastest-growing fields in AI. Natural language processing is the field that enables machines to understand, interpret, and generate human language, paving the way for human-machine interactions that were once limited to science fiction. At the heart of this ability is the practice of *"prompting"* a technique users use to steer AI models toward producing text that is both coherent and relevant in context [1]. Prompting is basically a communication technique that we use with AI. It consists of providing a specific input (a phrase, question, or command) to a language model, which produces an output based on that input. The input is called the *"prompt,"* and the generated text is the model's response. This mimics what humans also do: how you ask the question can change the answer you get [2].

Sumit Tripathi

Imagine someone is discussing a festive project with a coworker. If the inquiry is instead, *"What are your thoughts on our current marketing strategy?"* The person may gain an overall understanding of what they are thinking. But what if we asked, *"How can we improve our digital marketing efforts in the coming quarter?"* Most likely, the answer is more explicit and referable. When engaging with language models, the ambiguity or precision of the interaction cue, as in human conversation, influences the correspondence between the input and output. It is not only about asking questions; it is about getting the model up to the anticipated level of information. The prompt must be crafted accordingly, depending on whether the aim is to generate a creative story, write a technical document, or answer a complex question; the output highly depends on how well the prompt is written. That said, to leverage this tool effectively, one must understand the nuances of prompting.

THE DEEP AND WINDING ROAD TO A GREAT PROMPT

Prompting is a science as well as an art. The best results from a language model require a precise combination of creativity, linguistic intuition, and technical expertise. Prompt formulation is crucial because it directly impacts output quality. It takes creativity to go outside the box and to provide prompts that enable the model to offer novel and insightful solutions [3]. Linguistic intuition helps select the appropriate phrase, tone, and structure to ensure the model understands the query and provides an appropriate answer. Technical knowledge is essential, as understanding the model's capabilities and limitations enables you to improve prompts for maximum accuracy and relevance [4]. All of these elements interact to unlock the language model's potential, ensuring it provides responses that are not only correct but also relevant and insightful. Effective prompting relies on the following principles:

Clarity – Getting to the Point

The key to good prompting is clarity. A well-formed prompt reduces ambiguity; therefore, the model knows precisely what request it has received. If a prompt is vague or poorly constructed, the model may produce an output that is off-topic, incomplete, or nonsensical. As an example, take the prompt, *"What do you know about climate change?"* While this is an appropriate request, it is quite vague, and the responses might differ (*e.g.*, from causes of climate change to its impact on different ecosystems). A clearer, more focused prompt may be: *"Describe how human activity affects climate change."* In this example, the prompt is tailored to address a human factor; it can help the model understand what is going on and give a more relevant response. This focuses on instruction text generation for another example of how clarity matters. When you ask the model, *"How do I bake a cake?"* the answer could differ wildly based on how the model interprets the question. However, if you give the instruction, *"List a step-by-step recipe for baking a chocolate cake,"* the model will generate a more detailed, and probably more useful, set of instructions.

Clarity is not only an issue of syntax, but also of format — there are ways to ask a question that make it less likely to be misinterpreted. So, asking a question like, here's an example: *"What should I do about low sales?"* when looking for advice or a solution. It may be too open-ended, resulting in generic advice. Instead of a more general query like *"How do I increase my sales?"* which could lead to fluffing stuff like *"You can try Instagram or TikTok ads"*, you ask more specifically, *"What strategies can I implement to increase web sales of sustainable products?"* This steers the model towards more actionable and relevant advice.

Tip to Give Context to the Reader: Framing the Prompt

Context is a fundamental part that includes the background information for the model to provide an accurate answer. In the absence of this context, the model would probably generate a general response, one that is too abstract and generic. Adding a space before the prompt contextualizes the request and steers the model's writing output toward that particular situation. For instance, if you use a prompt like, *"Discuss the impact of technology,"* the result would likely be a generic answer. But when you add that context: *"Literature will be costly but here are all the ways I'm using technology that will affect remote work during the COVID-19 pandemic."* Adding context helps narrow it down, leading to more relevant and constructive output.

Contextual prompting is the critical factor, particularly within disciplines like law, medicine, or technical writing, where specificity and relevance are everything. A prompt like *"Describe the legal implications of data privacy"* has room for context: *"Describe the legal implications of data privacy for healthcare providers in the United States."* Here, you are not only improving the accuracy of the response but also ensuring the generated text is usable in your use case. Context is a key to creative applications. If, say, you give a model the prompt *"Write me a story,"* it'll spit out a generic story. But with context — *"Write a story set in a dystopian future in which humans have colonized Mars"* — the model will be nudged towards a more imaginative and contextually rich story.

Specificity: Defining the Context for Generating Accurate Outputs

Specificity works with clarity and with context: the more narrow the prompt, the more narrow the result. If the prompt is too general, the model has too much freedom, leading to possible outputs that may not serve the user. A question like *"What is AI?"* will encourage GPT to respond. However, the response will be superficial and generic in terms of artificial intelligence. While it may be useful for a beginner who knows nothing about the subject, the response lacks depth and detail. However, a more targeted, domain-specific query, such as *"What is the difference between supervised and unsupervised learning in AI?"* This will help to reduce the topic and provide a more focused and complete explanation. This type of challenge narrows the scope, pushing the model to shed light on certain areas of AI, such as machine learning paradigms, their distinctions, and applications [5]. This contrast emphasizes the necessity of using precise cues to elicit more relevant and informative replies from a language model.

One other area is in the field of creative writing. A prompt such as *"Write a story,"* lacks specificity and could result in any number of plotlines. But if you tell it, *"I want a story about a young girl who finds out she has magical powers,"* it pulls the model's focus toward writing a story that follows this narrative, creating a more cohesive and relevant story. Being specific also aids in creating technical content. For example, the prompt *"Explain quantum mechanics"* can yield a general overview of the topic, while the prompt *"Explain the concept of quantum entanglement in simple terms"* directs the model to produce a specific and easily understandable description.

The Iterative Refine: A Mighty Plan

Prompting is not often an ask-and-done task. Iterative refinement is often needed to get optimal results. You may not get the output you want on your first try at a prompt, and that's perfectly fine. Based on the answer provided by the language model, we need to keep refining the prompt step by step in order to improve the final output text. When the model is asked to *"Explain photosynthesis,"* and the response is too technical, the prompt can be modified to say, *"Explain how photosynthesis works in language a 10-year-old would understand."* By adding this context, the input is guided, leading to a response that is more accessible and better aligned with the expected output.

Iterative refinement is especially effective in more technical domains where precision is important. For example, if generating a code snippet from a prompt does not return the correct or optimal code, adding more detail to the prompt or constraints can help fine-tune the results. For example, some prompting, such as

"Generate a Python script using the quicksort algorithm to sort a list of integers," instead of *"Generate a Python script for sorting a list,"* adds the right hint to get the output we expect. Refinement also extends to creative tasks. Imagine a user gives a model the prompt *"Write a poem about love."* The user should make sure to ask for elaborations or deeper analysis. By narrowing the prompt—"Write a sonnet about the bittersweet nature of unrequited love"—the user will steer the model's output toward a more complex, stylistically fitting poem.

THEORIES OF PROMPTING IN WORK AND IN LIFE

Writing effective prompts is crucial for both academic and professional applications in a variety of domains. Precise prompts are a vital tool for academics, as they can guide the generation of research insights, summaries, and investigations of intricate concepts. Large language models have a broad range of potential uses in industry, ranging from data analysis and decision-making support to content creation and customer service automation. These models can generate outputs that are pertinent, actionable, and tailored to the demands of the sector when prompts are written well. The right design of well-structured prompts ensures LLMs provide their best and most contextually relevant answers, whether in marketing and customer engagement, healthcare and medical research, finance, or predictive analytics. The solutions and insights gained by perfecting the art of rapid engineering will unleash the full potential of LLMs and spur efficiency and innovation across various industries.

How to Get Started with Content Creation and Marketing

When it comes to content creation, prompting can be a useful technique for writing blog posts, articles, marketing content, and more. A marketer, for instancc, could input a prompt like *"Gcneratc a blog post on thc benefits of using solar energy"* to create an informative piece for readers. By specifying which demographic to target in the prompt — such as *"Write a blog post on the benefits of using solar energy for homeowners in urban areas"* —the output produced can be targeted to a specific demographic and thus perhaps be more relevant and engaging. In social media marketing, for instance, a good prompt could be iterated further: *"Generate a tweet to promote a new product launch"* becomes *"Generate a tweet to promote the launch of our eco-friendly water bottle, featuring sustainable materials and design."* Such a high level of specificity enables content to be in keeping with the brand's messaging and goals.

Iterative refinement processes help in content creation as well. This would help marketers improve their prompts and structure from the start: for example, if the first prompt doesn't spark interest in the output stream, a marketer could adjust the prompt and instead ask for a particular benefit or feature: *"Create a tweet and promote our eco-friendly water bottle, exactly the one that keeps drinks cold for 24 hours."* By further refining the tone and style, the model can produce increasingly persuasive content that engages with the intended audience.

Customer Service and Engagement

Prompting turns as a practical choice for automating customer service and communication. By using LLMs to provide responses to frequently asked customer inquiries, businesses can reduce the workload for human agents and speed up response times. A straightforward response could be obtained by using a prompt like *"Generate response to customer asking about return policy."* With the prompt being further refined to *"Generate a response to a customer asking about the return policy for items purchased during a sale,"* the output is more responsive to the specific scenario and more precisely calibrated. Similarly, one can use LLMs to customize replies according to customer information. Customize prompts, *e.g.*, a prompt such as *"Generate a response to a customer inquiring about the status of his recent order"* can be further tailored with specific details: *"Generate a response to John Doe inquiring about the status of order #12345, placed on June 15th."*

Tutoring and Educational Tools

Education is one of the fields where prompt engineering can generate teaching materials, practice questions, or even a simulated tutoring session. A teacher could start with *"Create a set of practice questions on the topic of fractions for 6th-grade students"* and get a set of questions that are grade-appropriate and curriculum aligned. Additionally, LLMs can enable the clarification of difficult ideas in more simplistic language, assisting students in understanding material in a more accessible way. For instance, educators can use the prompt *"Explain the idea of photosynthesis to a 5th grader,"* and it will generate an explanation that a fifth grader can understand, thus improving the learning experience.

Prompts are personalized learning opportunities for a tutor. *"Create a math quiz for a student who has difficulty with multiplication but does well with addition"* is an example of a prompt that enables the model to customize the content to meet the needs of the individual learner. A balanced and successful learning experience is ensured by this method, which offers practice that concentrates on the areas in which the learner struggles while simultaneously reiterating the ideas they already understand. Adaptive learning can also be beneficial in the educational tools. For instance, if a learner has difficulty with a certain concept, the tutor can narrow the prompting to that area: *"Create a set of practice questions for a 6th-grade student on multiplying fractions who has great difficulty with this concept."* This type of specificity helps solidify the student's comprehension and instill confidence.

The Legal and Technical Documentation

There are innumerable types of roles in which effective prompting adds great value (most notably for legal practitioners and technical authors). Legal writing prompts may generate contracts, legal opinions, or case law summaries. So, instead of a vague prompt like *"Draft a non-disclosure agreement for a software company,"* you can specify details like, *"Draft a non-disclosure agreement for a software company working with an external vendor, including clauses on data protection and intellectual property rights"*.

In technical documentation, prompt engineering can help create user manuals, API documentation, and troubleshooting guides. For example, a prompt like *"Write a user manual for a new smartphone"* can be improved to *"Write a user manual for a new smartphone, focusing on the setup process and key features for first-time users."* This way, the documentation can be clear, concise, and easily usable. Iterative refinement also applies to technical documentation. If, for example, the first output would be too technical for the audience, the prompt can be improved: *"Write a user manual for a new smartphone, concentrating on the setup process and key features, using language appropriate for non-technical users"*. This refinement not only helps ensure that the documentation is accessible but also easy enough to be followed.

Writing for Creative Studies and Storytelling

For writers and storytellers, prompting offers a path to new avenues of creativity. An effective prompt can get the words flowing when you're feeling stuck, whether you're writing a novel, a screenplay or a poem. *"Write a story about a detective in a futuristic city"* is a broad prompt that can elicit a variety of replies. Changing the prompt to *"Write a story about a detective in a futuristic city who uncovers a conspiracy involving artificial intelligence"* helps the model come up with a more focused and interesting plot. This results in a more complex tale with additional aspects like artificial intelligence and the conspiracy, making it more engaging.

Another idea is to prompt your way across genres or styles. Using the command, *'Write a poem about the ocean in the style of Emily Dickinson'*, combines creating a body of creative text (poem) with stylistic writing (using Dickinson's voice); enabling the writer to experiment with different writing voices, techniques, and forms. Iterative refinement serves creative writing well, too. If the initial output is too little emotionally, the prompt can be improved: *"Write a poem about the ocean in the style of Emily Dickinson about longing."* This revision focuses this piece more, allowing for more subtlety and depth.

AN INTRODUCTION TO LLMS (LARGE LANGUAGE MODELS) FOR GENERATING TEXT

The creation of LLMs is a major milestone in the history of AI and ML. Training data is obtained from these models, such as GPT-3, BERT, and T5, which interpret and generate human-readable text from prompts. LLMs have been trained on extensive datasets that include diverse forms of text from books, articles, websites, and other sources. This massive training enables them to produce information that is logical, contextually relevant, and quite often unrecognizable from human-written text.

Why Are LLMs So Powerful: The Transformers and Attention Mechanisms

The backbone of most LLMs is the transformer architecture, a type of neural network specification that has transformed the landscape of NLP. To begin with, the transformer model was first proposed in the article "Attention is All You Need" from Vaswani *et al.*, and then formed the base of many state-of-the-art language models [5]. The main innovation of the transformer model is its attention mechanisms, which let the model consider how important the different words in a sentence are to one another. This allows the model to better capture long-range dependencies in text, making it especially well-suited for understanding context and generating coherent responses. The most notable feature of transformers is their ability to process text in parallel as opposed to earlier models that processed text sequentially, leading to drastically better training efficiency and performance. This innovation enabled the architecting of LLMs with billions of parameters, which can now generate text with unprecedented fluency and accuracy [6].

The Training Process: Data, Computation, and Fine-tuning

This is done by feeding the LLM immense amounts of data, enabling the model to discern linguistic patterns, structures, and associations. During this process, the model consumes significant computational resources, as it scans and performs analysis of billions of words to 'build' its lexicon. This is because the training itself starts with pre-training, where we teach the model how to predict the next word given the words before it. This exercise, called language modelling, allows the model to gain expertise in syntax, grammar, and semantics. Pre-training is followed by fine-tuning, in which the model is adapted for certain tasks or domains. This training is often preceded by further training, called fine-tuning, on a narrower domain dataset closer to the application [7]. More refined models, or the results of fine-tuning on specific datasets, we might imagine that a model could be fine-tuned on medical texts and be better able to generate medically accurate and clinically relevant content based on a prompt in the healthcare space.

GPT-4 and Beyond: What Does the Future Hold for LLMs

The evolution of large language models (LLMs) has been characterized by fast-paced progression in both model architecture and training methodologies. Perhaps the most significant evolution in this area is the evolution from GPT-3 to GPT-4, a monumental leap in capability and performance [8].

GPT-3 by OpenAI

When GPT-3, created by OpenAI, was released, it was one of the biggest and most powerful language models yet. GPT-3, with 175 billion parameters, could also do a lot: answer questions, write essays, generate code or poetry. It was widely used among developers and researchers due to its versatility. For instance, a developer could use GPT-3 to build an AI-powered writing assistant that helps the user write emails, articles, or even full-fledged books. With a proper prompt, the assistant can generate text that mimics the style and intent of the individual who prompted it.

GPT-4 by OpenAI

GPT-4, an advanced model of GPT-3, was introduced by OpenAI, capitalizing on the previous model's milestones, with expanded capabilities in precision, contextual comprehension, and the capacity to complete intricate tasks. GPT-4 — which boasts even more parameters than GPT-3 — is at the frontiers of what AI-driven text generation can achieve. GPT-4 is accessible through OpenAI's API, similar to GPT-3, and has been integrated into a variety of applications, ranging from advanced virtual assistants to sophisticated content creation tools. Its enhanced capabilities make it suitable for a wider range of applications, including those requiring detailed analysis, creativity, and critical thinking. To illustrate, one might feed GPT-4 an enormous dataset of academic papers to distill the key findings and trends across a number of studies, a task that can save precious hours and improve the breadth of their coverage [9].

Gemini by Google

And Gemini, the most recent iteration of generative AI from Google, is a state-o--the-art large language model that promises to provide functionality across various Natural Language Processing (NLP) use cases. Gemini unifies the best of previous language models (like BERT and T5) and incorporates benefits from recent developments in multimodal learning so that it can take in and produce text based on images, audio, and other types of information. The ability of Gemini to process multimodal inputs makes it especially useful in applications that may require more than just plain text, such as interactive AI applications, digital media production and the like. By issuing Gemini *via* the Integrity cloud and other services, Google opened up this powerful tool to developers and researchers who want to build the next class of AI apps.

Using Gemini, a media organization may provide interactive content that smoothly combines text, images, and audio. The storytelling experience is improved using this method, making it more captivating and immersive for online viewers. The business may provide viewers with dynamic content that connects with them on a deeper level by fusing several media types, which enables them to engage with and experience the story in a more engaging and customized manner. Multimedia integration has the power to significantly alter conventional narrative and increase the impact of digital content.

PUBLICLY AVAILABLE LLMS: THE MOST POWERFUL AI AVAILABLE

Although creating and using LLMs may take up resources, many groups have made those models available to the public, which places the potent AI gear within reach of the average person. These are some of the most popular publicly available LLMs:

BERT by Google

Another particularly LLM that had a great impact on the field is BERT (Bidirectional Encoder Representations from Transformers), developed by Google. Whereas GPT-3 is a generative model, BERT is used mainly for text classification, sentiment analysis, and question answering.

By training on both directions at once, BERT learns a word from both a forward and backward perspective, which is extremely useful for tasks that depend on a deep understanding of the relationship and context of words within sentences. For the NLP community, Google has open-sourced BERT *via* its TensorFlow Hub, which allows researchers and developers to fine-tune the model for a range of NLP tasks. A simple case: A company may use BERT to improve its search engine, so that it better comprehends user queries and provides more appropriate results.

T5 by Google

Can we feed T5 data with another language and expect to get used to it? T5 converts all NLP tasks into text-to-text format, allowing both input and output to be represented as text strings. T5 can convert any text-based task into a text-t--text format. T5 is open source (available on GitHub) by Google. It has become well known for a variety of applications due to its versatility and power. For instance, a developer could leverage T5 to develop an AI tool that automatically shortens lengthy articles or documents into clear, easy-to-read summaries, making life easier for users.

RoBERTa by Facebook AI

RoBERTa (Robustly optimized BERT approach) is a Facebook AI developed variant of BERT. By pre-training on vastly larger batches than in BERT, RoBERTa takes a bite out of everything, and a new study shows it is better suited for human language understanding (or NLP). RoBERTa is pre-trained on massive datasets available for direct use *via* the Hugging Face model repository, where you can find other models to fine-tune on further tasks. For instance, an organization can apply RoBERTa to create a tool that performs sentiment analysis for what people are saying about them on social media, allowing them to quickly address customer feedback.

XLNet by Google/CMU

XLNet is another powerful LLM that combines the best features of both BERT and autoregressive models such as GPT. It employs a permutation-based training approach, enabling it to learn bidirectional context, as well as the dependencies among words. XLNet has performed well on several NLP benchmarks and is available for use on TensorFlow Hub, among other places. XLNet could be used by researchers to create more accurate language models in specialized domains (*e.g.*, legal or medical texts), which require understanding complex dependencies.

ETHICAL IMPLICATIONS AND CHALLENGES

LLMs have their challenges, despite their many advantages. One major cause of concern is biases, since these models are based on trained data, which can come with built-in biases. This results in potential inaccuracies and bias, producing inappropriate content, though it also depends on the prompt and sometimes sensitive topics. To begin with, LLMs are versatile but operate as a *"black box."* Although these models can produce impressive results, interpreting how they reach specific outputs is frequently challenging. Such opacity can be problematic for accountability and trust, especially in areas such as healthcare or the law, where the stakes of erroneous or biased outputs can be high [10].

Researchers and developers are working on techniques to combat these issues, including making LLMs fairer, more transparent, and more accountable. This includes not only developing tools to identify and mitigate bias, but also creating them so people can use them to understand how the model arrived at what it generates.

THE FUTURE OF LLMS: BROADER APPLICATIONS AND ENHANCED CAPABILITIES

The applications of LLMs are set to grow even larger as their development progresses. Improving AI models is anticipated based on the developments in AI analysis research. The type of work we do may involve much more integration of LLMs, and it's also likely that LLMs will become embedded deeper into our day-to-day lives, for instance, in personalized education or learning, healthcare, artistic creation or storytelling. [news_english]From generating personalized learning experiences for students to creating tailored healthcare advice based on individual medical histories, LLMs can be utilized to fill in certain gaps in human writing — even co-writing works with humans, and writing screenplays with people.

Additionally, continued research on AI ethics and fairness will mitigate some of the existing issues with LLMs, allowing them to become more reliable and responsible text generation tools. As these models become more powerful, they will play a crucial role in redefining the way we communicate, create, and interact with technology.

In the domain of text generation powered by AI, prompting and LLMs are a match made in heaven. However, by embracing the core tenets of effective prompting — clarity in communication, context provided, specificity requested, and iterative refining — users can unlock the true power of LLMs, creating output not just that is accurate, but also creative, engaging and pertinent. This list will keep growing as LLMs continue to evolve, enabling innovations in even more fields. If you're a writer, a researcher, a business professional, or just someone who is curious about the power of AI, learning to prompt effectively and having an understanding of the fundamentals of LLMs will provide you with the skills to make good use of AI for generating quality text. But by thinking of prompting as an art and a science, and through exploiting the unique capabilities of LLMs, you can get remarkable content out of them for your needs, whatever it might be; a novel, a legal document, a social media post, you name it. With proper usage, we all have a bright future in text generation.

CONCLUSION

The need of learning the craft of prompting for users who want to properly employ AI language models is emphasized in this chapter. Users' interactions with AI models depend on how well-defined, contextually relevant, and clear the instructions are. In order to maximize their outputs, users must adjust to the advantages and disadvantages of AI systems like GPT-4 and Gemini as they develop further. The potential of AI language models in fields such as content creation, customer service, education, and legal documentation presents vast opportunities for innovation, enabling industries to enhance productivity and decision-making. However, the ethical challenges of AI, such as bias and opacity, must be addressed to ensure responsible use. Ultimately, a deeper understanding of how to craft effective prompts, coupled with knowledge of the underlying technology, will allow users to harness the full power of AI for a wide range of applications, from academic research to creative endeavours. The chapter calls for an ongoing exploration of this dynamic field to maximize the benefits of AI-driven text generation in various industries.

REFERENCES

[1] D. Khurana, A. Koli, K. Khatter, and S. Singh, "Natural language processing: State of the art, current trends and challenges", *Multimedia Tools Appl.,* vol. 82, no. 3, pp. 3713-3744, 2023. [http://dx.doi.org/10.1007/s11042-022-13428-4] [PMID: 35855771]

[2] R. He, A. Ravula, B. Kanagal, and J. Ainslie, "RealFormer: Transformer likes residual attention," in *Findings of the Association for Computational Linguistics: ACL-IJCNLP 2021*, C. Zong, F. Xia, W. Li, and R. Navigli, Eds. *Online: Association for Computational Linguistics*, 2021, pp. 929–943. [http://dx.doi.org/10.18653/v1/2021.findings-acl.81]

[3] P. Sahoo, A.K. Singh, S. Saha, V. Jain, S. Mondal, and A. Chadha, "A systematic survey of prompt engineering in large language models: Techniques and applications", *arXiv:2402.07927*, Feb. 05, 2024. [http://dx.doi.org/10.48550/arXiv.2402.07927]

[4] B. Chen, Z. Zhang, N. Langrené, and S. Zhu, "Unleashing the potential of prompt engineering in large language models: A comprehensive review", Sep. 05, 2024. [http://dx.doi.org/10.48550/arXiv.2310.14735]

[5] A. Vaswani, N. Shazeer, N. Parmar, J. Uszkoreit, L. Jones, A. N. Gomez, Ł. Kaiser, and I. Polosukhin, "Attention is all you need," *arXiv:1706.03762*, Jun. 12, 2017. Available: http://arxiv.org/abs/1706.03762

[6] Z. Niu, G. Zhong, and H. Yu, "A review on the attention mechanism of deep learning", *Neurocomputing,* vol. 452, pp. 48-62, 2021. [http://dx.doi.org/10.1016/j.neucom.2021.03.091]

[7] X. Wang, M. Tang, T. Yang, and Z. Wang, "A novel network with multiple attention mechanisms for aspect-level sentiment analysis", *Knowl. Base. Syst.,* vol. 227, 2021.107196 [http://dx.doi.org/10.1016/j.knosys.2021.107196]

[8] G. Yenduri, "Generative pre-trained transformer: A comprehensive review on enabling technologies, potential applications, emerging challenges, and future directions", May 21, 2023. [http://dx.doi.org/10.48550/arXiv.2305.10435]

[9] P.P. Ray, "ChatGPT: A comprehensive review on background, applications, key challenges, bias, ethics, limitations and future scope", *Internet of Things and Cyber-Physical Systems,* vol. 3, pp. 121-154, 2023. [http://dx.doi.org/10.1016/j.iotcps.2023.04.003]

[10] J.C.L. Ong, S.Y.H. Chang, W. William, A.J. Butte, N.H. Shah, L.S.T. Chew, N. Liu, F. Doshi-Velez, W. Lu, J. Savulescu, and D.S.W. Ting, "Ethical and regulatory challenges of large language models in medicine", *Lancet Digit. Health,* vol. 6, no. 6, pp. e428-e432, 2024. [http://dx.doi.org/10.1016/S2589-7500(24)00061-X] [PMID: 38658283]

CHAPTER 2

Unveiling the Potential: Large Language Models

Abstract: This chapter discusses Large Language Models (LLMs) and their tremendous use in natural language processing (NLP). It begins by discussing how LLMs are created. It focuses on aspects such as spatial encodings, neural network layers, and attention techniques that enable these models to sound more human. Next, it examines how the transformer architecture works. This is the base of most LLMs today. The chapter explains multi-head attention and self-attention. These help the models understand long sentences and the context around words. The chapter also covers how LLMs are trained. First, they go through pre-training. This helps them learn general language by using large datasets. Then comes fine-tuning, where the models focus on specific tasks. Additionally, it discusses where LLMs are used, such as in chatbots, content generation, and translation services. In the end, it highlights how LLMs are changing industries like education, healthcare, and writing.

Keywords: Attention mechanisms, Large Language Models (LLMs), Neural networks, Natural Language Processing (NLP), Positional encodings, Transformer architecture.

INTRODUCTION

In recent times, the domain of artificial intelligence has witnessed the rise of Large Language Models (LLMs), transformative agents that have redefined the landscape of natural language processing. These ultra-powerful language models are hailed as the pinnacle of linguistic AI. In this chapter, we embark on an enlightening exploration of the intricacies of LLMs — their sophisticated architecture, complex training methodologies, and wide-ranging applications that challenge the traditional limitations of language-based interactions [1]. The LLMs are at the crux of problem-solving and the creative end ever since the digital era began unfolding. The alternative approaches pattern stands at the centre of this exploration, a multi-use tool that turns this into a dynamic process between intelligent people. Indeed, this template is a priceless compass, sailing users through the content ocean that lives inside LLMs and catapulting them into being a cog in a creative wheel working in tandem with LLMs.

Sumit Tripathi

UNDERSTANDING THE ARCHITECTURE

Large language models (LLMs) are complex frameworks with a range of interconnected aspects that are explicitly designed to mimic the intricate understanding of human language. The "maze" above is a simplified version of how it looks when you are building a Model. As we visualize this architecture through a rich block diagram, we get a highly structured roadmap; we can navigate the architecture's complexity by looking at it. It must be a language model, as we are also told that a large part of the neural network is composed of a transformer encoder-decoder, as described in the research papers [2]. With this visualization, we can start to see beyond the complex black box that is LLMs and appreciate the nuanced mechanics behind their astounding language processing capabilities.

Attention Mechanisms: Charting the Contextual Waters

Attention is a key component of Large Language Models (LLMs) that allows the model to attend to the large context of language. Hence, you can picture the attention mechanism exactly as a navigation route that helps our model to sail through the complex ocean of language. Similar to a sailor using a compass to guide them toward specific landmarks or directions, this attention mechanism can help the model focus on relevant aspects of an input sequence. This selective attention mimics the nuanced attention observed in human cognition. Similar to how humans naturally pay attention to particular elements of a conversation or text, determined by context and relevance, LLMs rely on attention mechanisms: they assign importance to specific elements of the input sequence while generating the output. It helps the model focus on the most relevant pieces of information and encode them into numerical vectors that it can learn from to improve its ability to generate coherent writing.

This is possible because, by dynamically turning its attention up and down in context, an LLM can learn how textual structures and subtleties work in a particular environment and produce results that are precise and contextually appropriate. By allowing the model to focus on relevant context while generating text, the attention mechanism allows LLMs to effectively imitate the complex reflective processes in human language understanding, which is why they become a powerful resource for LLMs to create high-quality text. Attention helps associate words between source and target sentences in translation, giving more weight to contextually meaningful words and leading them to align more closely. But listening to idioms requires paying attention to get the meaning.

Neural Network Layers: From Top to Bottom

One specific aspect of LLM architecture stands out: the multilayer arrangement of neural networks that work together to improve the model's ability to create complex representations of linguistic subtleties. These layers allow the model to learn different levels of abstraction, from the basic token representations to more complex language patterns. The neural network is composed of multiple layers, each designed to extract different features and information from the raw input data [3]. The early layers learn basic elements and patterns, with deeper layers using that knowledge to produce higher-order and more abstract representations of language. This staged methodology allows the model to understand hierarchical connections within the information, progressively evolving crude input into an advanced and multifaceted symbolic portrayal [4]. However, the structure of LLMs is highly hierarchical, where each stage in the processing chain represents a refinement of the data through cascading transformations. Not only can the model currently understand basic syntactic and semantic structures, but it can also identify many of the more subtle nuances, idioms, and context-dependent meanings in language. This stacked organizational structure is one of the contributing factors that allow the LLM to understand and generate human-like text at an incredible scale and proficiency, which is what makes it such a powerful information retrieval and text synthesis engine.

A Practical Example: For an application like sentiment analysis, such layers work together in comprehensively examining those words that carry sentiments and record the subtle changes in sentiments over a complete text. Variation in the depth of neural layers allows the model to be sensitive to different emotional tones.

Positional Encodings: Navigating Through the Importance of Sequence

Let's try to tackle this carefully in the context of natural language processing: because language is (typically) sequential in nature, positional encodings are what provide a sense of order to the raw context. These encodings are significant as they provide the model third-party information about the location of words in a sentence. In other words, they serve as milestones that help the model understand the contextual relevance of the order of words. Since language is sequenced over time, and relies on the ordering of words for meaning, positional encodings provide the clip of temporal context needed. Positional Awareness: They allow the model to recognize not just the words in order of a sequence but also their relationships with one another according to positioning. This allows for a mapping to be made between elements of a sentence that can differ in priority, intonation, or order in terms of when they occurred.

It is then able to learn how to move around the language space and represent the sequential nature of language by adding positional encodings specifically into the architecture of the model. This, conversely, improves the model's ability to perform on targeted tasks, which validate its functionality in language understanding, translation, and generation, which means there are specific aspects of the learned function that improve its functioning.

Example from the Real World: Think of the sentences "Apple is a company" and "A company is an apple." Without positional encodings, the model might find it hard to differentiate between them, as the arrangement of words is crucial to communicating the specific message.

Transformer Architecture: The Language Conductors

At the heart of Large Language Models (LLMs) lies the transformer architecture, a composition of attention mechanisms and neural layers harmonizing to create a symphony of linguistic understanding. They revolutionized the field of language processing with their Transform Architecture, which enabled parallelization and capture of long-range dependencies in sequences of words. The attention mechanisms that the transformer uses are the virtuoso conductors of this symphony of language. They introduce an element of selective attention by allowing the model to focus on certain parts of the input sequence, spanning a wide range of input sequences in a way that mirrors human attention. This selective focus allows the model to attend to multiple instances of data simultaneously, improving efficiency and allowing computations to be parallelized. As a result, not only does the transformer architecture leverage the sequential nature of language, but it also enables parallel processing, providing substantial gains in training and inference time. In addition, the neural layers of the transformer integrate to develop non-linear features that can properties on complex structures of language. All of these layers work in parallel, enabling the model to efficiently capture and utilize contextual information across positions in the sequence. By leveraging self-attention, the transformer can weigh the importance of different words relative to one another, regardless of their distance in the input sequence, thus handling long-range dependencies better than traditional RNN models.

More precisely, the transformer architecture embedded in the architecture of LLMs is a revolutionary idea that arranges and formulates a language with unprecedented freedom. This approach has revolutionized the field of language processing, leading to LLMs that achieve unprecedented levels of sophistication and proficiency at tasks like natural language understanding, generation, and translation, through their capacity to parallelize computations and model long-range dependencies in textual data.

Example from real life: In language modelling tasks, it was necessary to catch dependencies between words far beyond their vicinity, giving the model the power to generate coherent and contextually rich outputs.

We delve into the intricacies of these components in the architecture of LLMs to understand how they unlock the dynamics of language and propel the innovative applications and solving paradigms in ways yet to be imagined. In the coming sections, we will take a closer look at the training methods that transform these models into beacons of language prowess.

TRAINING METHODOLOGIES

The quality of an LLM depends particularly on how it has been trained, and one of the leading paradigms in this realm was the pre-trained/fine-tuned paradigm. This process arrives in two steps–one is pre-training, which helps learn general language based on a huge corpus of various textual data. This general knowledge is subsequently focused and adjusted through training on a smaller dataset that is more relevant to the task, optimizing its proficiency in a specific area.

Pre-training

Comprehensive Information

Exposure to large datasets, including a variety of language examples, is the initial step in pre training LLMs. This allows the models to acquire a general understanding of language, syntax, semantics, and world knowledge. Books, articles, webpages, and other text-based resources covering a wide range of subjects, genres, and writing styles are typically included in this extensive training set. Instead of attempting to complete a specific task, the goal of this stage is to acquire a fundamental understanding of language patterns. It focuses on understanding syntax rules, which include knowledge about how grammar and sentence construction are related. Additionally, by absorbing world knowledge from the data it encounters, the model will be able to comprehend common facts, ideas, and relationships between entities. By processing language in parallel and accounting for long-range dependencies between words, this architecture—which is at the heart of many contemporary LLMs—is excellent at capturing these kinds of patterns. It gives the model the capacity to comprehend intricate sentence structures and ascertain how words and phrases relate to one another in various contexts.

Analytical Transformation

The model gains a fundamental understanding of linguistic subtleties through training on this enormous volume of text data. The model can integrate linguistic nuances including tone, colloquial idioms, and context-dependent meanings thanks to this intensive training. This paradigm fosters the capacity to handle sentence structure variations, evaluate ambiguous language, and comprehend how words can change meaning based on context. Thus, in addition to learning how to generate grammatically sound text, the model also learns how to recognize and apply sophisticated linguistic notions like wordplay, metaphor, and sentiment nuance. This pre-training phase ensures that the model can handle a wide range of language-related activities; subsequent fine-tuning or task-specific training may then enable it to perform even better.

Fine-tuning

After pre-training, LLMs undergo fine-tuning to optimize their performance for a certain job or domain. This process of fine-tuning is crucial because it makes the model more suitable for a certain set of applications. In order to attain precision and relevance with the responses offered for domain-specific inquiries or problems, fine-tuning allows the model to focus on a small range of subjects or issue domains, whereas pre-training gives the model a broad view of the language. This stage involves fine-tuning the model on a specialized dataset, which may include technical articles, legal materials, or medical literature, depending on the task at hand. The goal of fine-tuning is to adjust the model's knowledge to the specific domain's complexities, improving its performance in areas where it must demonstrate competence.

As an example, the first model in Transfer Learning lacks the special nuances needed for a given sector because it was trained on a broader and broader language dataset. By fine-tuning, the model can apply its general knowledge of language while honing its specialized knowledge, increasing its ability to produce accurate and contextually relevant outcomes for that domain. Compared to training from scratch, this method not only improves the model's performance but also reduces the quantity of data required to train it for particular tasks.

Practical Applications

LLMs have a broad range of applications in various domains, reshaping human-computer interactions and creative endeavours. Some seminal examples highlighted their adaptability and efficacy:

Chatbots and Virtual Assistants

Explanation in Detail: LLMs provide the guiding principles for conversational agents by understanding user queries and producing contextually appropriate responses. Dynamic engagement converts user conversations into smooth, human-like discussions with the model. ChatGPT, an LLM-based trainer chatbot, serves as a model for real-world applications, able to respond in ways that energize and develop the conversation.

Content Generation

Extended Insight: The generative capacity of LLMs to produce coherent and contextually appropriate material carries numerous ramifications for their applications across various domains of creative activity, writing style, and as an instrument for summarization. These models make for valuable tool in the world of creativity.

Real World Example: Capturing GPT-3's creative writing prowess, the machine can spin poetry, stories, and articles with an incredibly varied assortment of tone and style—highlighting the versatility of the model.

Translation Services

LLMs are great translators, they convert text from one language to another preserving complicated elements of context. By integrating attention mechanisms into seq2seq models, the translation output becomes increasingly accurate and fluent.

Translating Real World Scenario: Google uses transformer-based translation with an attention mechanism that aligns multiple paragraph words to make quality translations in both directions.

Large Language Models deserve their own exploration, as they are capable of magic. By getting to grips with the complex architecture, subtle training techniques, and numerous use cases, it enables practitioners to maximize the potential of LLMs in a wide range of fields. With LLMs being a constantly progressing field, it is expected to push the limits of what is possible with linguistic AI beyond anything we can imagine.

LARGE LANGUAGE MODELS (LLMS) OF GOOGLE

The backbone of most LLMs, such as the one illustrated in Fig. (**1**), is the Transformer architecture, an exceptional architecture introduced by Vaswani *et al.*, in the paper "Attention is All You Need" released by Google in 2017. It was a game-changer for natural language processing and laid the groundwork for many future language architectures, such as BERT, GPT, and so on [5].

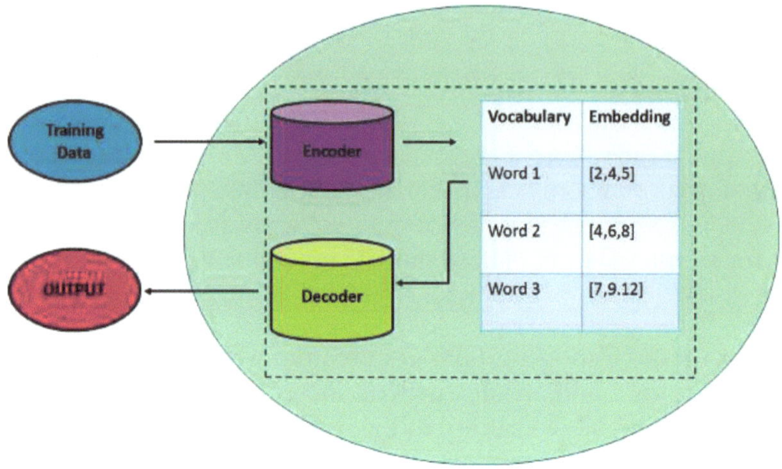

Fig. (1). Transformer model.

Special attention mechanisms make it possible for the model to weigh the importance of different parts of the input sequence, capturing contextual dependencies effectively. The key components can be summarized with a few more details as follows:

Self-Attention Mechanism

One of the most important innovations is the self-attention mechanism introduced with the Transformer architecture, allowing each word in the input sequence to look at the other words dynamically and weigh their importance based on relative context. This mechanism is an essential aspect of modelling complex relationships between words, regardless of their positions in the sequence. This approach differs from classic sequential models, in which words are processed one after the other; in self-attention, the Transformer is able to concurrently assess how important each word is in context to all the other words in the sequence [6]. Such a context-aware approach provides the model a mechanism to grasp word dependencies/correlations irrespective of their positions. This enables the model to learn the full semantic and syntactic relationships in the whole input sequence.

Practically speaking, it also allows the Transformer to better understand the context of a large piece of text, learn to maintain long-term dependencies, and ultimately to generate more coherent and contextual text. In short, self-attention is a key feature that made Transformer widely successful for tasks in natural language processing such as translation, summarization, and language comprehension. For example: In translation tasks, self-attention helps the model to correctly align words from the source language to the words in the target language, resulting in accurate and meaningful translations.

Multi-head Attention

Multi-head attention is used so that the model can learn to focus on different parts of the input sequence; it runs the self-attention mechanism in parallel on multiple heads. It allows the model to attend to different portions of the input at the same time, supporting a more subtle representation of the information in question. Multi-head attention applies so that each head attends to different features, allowing the model to learn a wide range of relationships in the sequence. Whereas its parallelized attention mechanism also enhances its versatility by allowing it to capture a wider range of features and contextual information, which helps to boost its performance across various natural language processing tasks.

Take a real-world example: Different heads can focus on different (sentiment-carrying) words in a sentence when analysing the sentiment; each head gives a little bit of contribution to the in-depth understanding of the overall sentiment.

Positional Encoding

Unlike classical recurrent neural networks, which are intrinsically aware of the order of their sequence, transformers do not have this inherent sequence awareness. To overcome this limitation, a new component, the positional encodings, is added. They provide information about the position of words in a sequence, allowing the model to learn sequential relationships. Now, to make the transformer aware of the word order, positional encodings are introduced because the self-attention mechanism, used in the transformer, is not aware of the position of each word. Positional encodings enable the model to effectively learn the ordered structure present in language inputs, helping it to understand and learn the underlying patterns of dependency and contextual meaning that vary depending on the arrangement of words in a context [7]. It helps maintain that sequential context for transformers, allowing them to perform well on tasks involving sequence data, such as language processing and observation. Sequential position information is strategically included through various methods in transformer architectures, which enables a better understanding of the ordering of data elements and enhances the model's ability to learn from such inputs.

Real-world Example: In language tasks, positional encoding helps identify which of "I love you" and "you love me" is either, since the order of the words matters to convey meaning.

Fig. (**2**) depicts the concept of embeddings in prompt engineering, a key technique in natural language processing (NLP). In this figure, various phrases such as "Lion," "Cub," "Chair," and "Leopard" are represented in a shared vector space, with each term assigned a vector. Such vectors are then subdivided into a multidimensional space, preferably a high-dimensional space, from which a machine learning model may understand the word relation in meaning. The box illustrated here symbolizes three dimensions, which represent this type of space in Fig. (**2**). Each vector represents a phrase, and the proximity and direction of the vectors shown on this diagram reveal the semantic links between the words. For example, "Lion" and "Cub" are closely connected, as seen by the arrows pointing in similar directions. This implies that they are semantically comparable, as a "Cub" is the child of a "Lion." This closeness in the embedding space exemplifies how word embeddings capture word relationships based on meanings, contexts, and affiliations. In comparison, the phrase "Chair" is further away from "Lion" and "Leopard," showing that it is semantically less linked to the other two names, which refer to the same group of wild creatures.

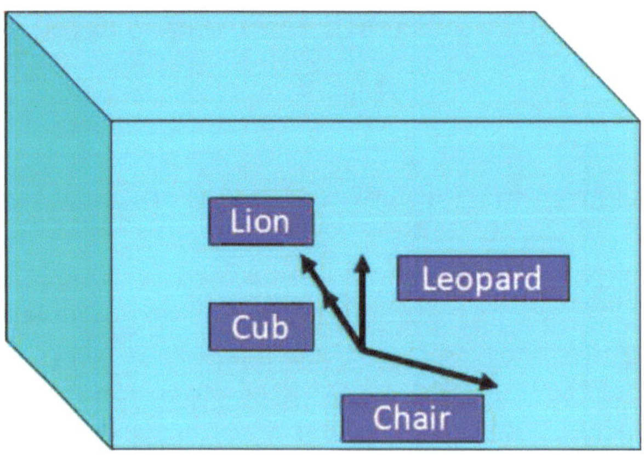

Fig. (2). Embeddings in LLMs.

A further intriguing aspect of word embeddings is that the arrows connecting words in the diagram indicate directional linkages. If the arrows between words point in the same direction, they are likely to have similar meanings or conceptual categories; if the arrows point in opposite ways, the words are less likely to be related. This feature of word embeddings is extremely essential in prompt engineering since embeddings assist machine learning models in understanding the differences between words, sentences, and concepts. By encoding language in this vector space, models can interpret, compare, and synthesize text with a better knowledge of word meanings and linkages [8].

Transformer Blocks

It is made up of 6 layers that include self-attention and a feedforward neural network. The blocks are stacked repetitively as blocks of blocks, giving the model a deep hierarchical structure. By stacking these layers, the model can learn complex patterns and relationships in the data at different levels of abstraction. Every block functions as an independent component, encompassing self-attention structures for grasping contextual associations and feedforward neural networks for refining and manipulating the processed representations. These blocks can be stacked to allow the model to go deeper into the working of language and learn hierarchical transformations of features. Hierarchical economy means that the model learns representations starting from basic.

Overall this stacking of building blocks is done repeatedly to give a high level layered architecture to the transformer model and allows it to learn complex inter-relationships in the language data. These multi-head self-attention layers, organized in a hierarchical manner, are instrumental in making Transformers successful for a broad range of natural language processing tasks, as they capture different levels of semantics and can effectively learn the nuances of human language.

For summarizing jobs, where the model runs through and summarizes similar content from various sections of a document, the hierarchical structure is more helpful. By determining the connections between sections or paragraphs, the model will then be able to efficiently condense the material while maintaining its key ideas and context. This helps to create a succinct yet thorough review of the full work by ensuring that the summary is logical and covers important concepts and ideas from different sections.

Residual Connections and Layer Normalization

A key design choice is made in the Transformer architecture to stabilize training and allow gradients to flow easily through deep networks. Layer normalization and a residual connection are added after each sub-layer in the Transformer block. This architecture arrangement is one of the key factors that allowed for the effective training of deeper models. As networks become deeper and deeper, it also helps us in forwarding propagation across networks by reducing the vanishing or exploding gradients problem. This normalization step helps attain and maintain robustness throughout the training step, so joint practice across different layers occurs with the added benefit of residual connection for better training stability. These connections allow the gradient to flow more easily without being blocked or saturated, effectively creating a shortcut for the gradient flow. This alleviates the difficulties of training extremely deep networks, since the network can learn identity mappings more easily, which helps the optimization process converge.

Either component enhances the stability of training deep Transformer models independently, and combined, they play a significant role in improving training efficacy. The stack of layers flows through dense communication, and the power of depth is preserved. This was a critical move, and its success has led to deep networks being used as powerful behaviour divers for new languages.

Reasons for these Components and How They Help in the Real World: Across the layers, those small steps such as layer normalization and residual connections facilitate the capability to solve various kinds of queries in the complex language understanding tasks, like in question answering tasks.

The Transformer Architecture: the usual starting point is the original "Attention is All You Need" paper; a fundamental understanding of how Large Language Models (LLMs) process language. A transformative departure from the past, this paper established the base for a new paradigm in natural language processing -- one in which attention mechanisms take precedence over recurrent or convolutional structures. Studying the architecture of a Transformer as specified in this document can reveal how LLMs understand and produce language using complex patterns. By linking the underlying principles of LLMs to the transformer architecture, we build a framework to better understand the advances needed to build powerful and context-aware language models in the future. It highlights the utilization of attention mechanisms, which allow the model to dynamically weigh different parts of the input based on their relevance to the task at hand. With this understanding in hand, researchers and practitioners can continue to innovate and improve on language models, advancing the state of natural language understanding and generation.

CONCLUSION

Large Language Models' (LLMs') enormous potential in natural language processing (NLP) is discussed in this chapter. It begins with an explanation of how LLMs operate. Important components that enable these models to speak like humans are highlighted, including positional encodings, neural networks, and attention techniques. The architecture of the transformer is dissected in this chapter. For most LLMs, this framework is essential. It demonstrates how the models are able to comprehend speech across vast distances and maintain context by using features like multi-head attention and self-attention. It then discusses the training process for LLMs. In order to understand linguistic patterns, the model must first learn from vast volumes of data during the pre-training phase. During fine-tuning, the model improves at particular tasks. Practical applications of LLMs are also covered in this chapter. These include chatbots, creating content, and translation services. In the end, it talks about how LLMs are changing areas like education, healthcare, and creative writing. With the transformer setup, LLMs have changed the game for how computers handle language. Their features make them great for tasks like text generation and translation. The training process helps them work well in different situations. However, challenges like needing a lot of computing power and keeping ethics in check still exist. As LLMs get better, they can improve communication and creativity in many fields, including education and customer service. The chapter encourages more innovation to make the most of LLMs while tackling their challenges.

REFERENCES

[1] H. Naveed, A. U. Khan, S. Qiu, M. Saqib, S. Anwar, M. Usman, N. Akhtar, N. Barnes, and A. Mian, "A comprehensive overview of large language models", Oct. 17, 2024. [http://dx.doi.org/10.48550/arXiv.2307.06435]

[2] Y. Yao, J. Duan, K. Xu, Y. Cai, Z. Sun, and Y. Zhang, "A survey on large language model (LLM) security and privacy: The Good, The Bad, and The Ugly", *High-Confidence Computing,* vol. 4, no. 2, p. 100211, 2024. [http://dx.doi.org/10.1016/j.hcc.2024.100211]

[3] M.U. Nasir, S. Earle, C. Cleghorn, S. James, and J. Togelius, "LLMatic: Neural architecture search *via* large language models and quality diversity optimization", in *Proceedings of the Genetic and Evolutionary Computation Conference (GECCO '24)*, Melbourne, VIC, Australia, 2024, pp. 1110–1118. [http://dx.doi.org/10.1145/3638529.3654017]

[4] M.F. Romano, L.C. Shih, I.C. Paschalidis, R. Au, and V.B. Kolachalama, "Large language models in neurology research and future practice", *Neurology,* vol. 101, no. 23, pp. 1058-1067, 2023. [http://dx.doi.org/10.1212/WNL.0000000000207967] [PMID: 37816646]

[5] J. Devlin, M-W. Chang, K. Lee, and K. Toutanova, "BERT: Pre-training of deep bidirectional transformers for language understanding", May 24, 2019. [http://dx.doi.org/10.48550/arXiv.1810.04805]

[6] C. Raffel, "Exploring the limits of transfer learning with a unified text-to-text transformer", Sep. 19, 2023. [http://dx.doi.org/10.48550/arXiv.1910.10683]

[7] K. Zhou, J. Yang, C.C. Loy, and Z. Liu, "Learning to prompt for vision-language models", *Int. J. Comput. Vis.,* vol. 130, no. 9, pp. 2337-2348, 2022. [http://dx.doi.org/10.1007/s11263-022-01653-1]

[8] N.M. Foumani, C.W. Tan, G.I. Webb, and M. Salehi, "Improving position encoding of transformers for multivariate time series classification", *Data Min. Knowl. Discov.,* vol. 38, no. 1, pp. 22-48, 2024. [http://dx.doi.org/10.1007/s10618-023-00948-2]

CHAPTER 3

Tokenization in Large Language Models (LLMs)

Abstract: In Natural Language Processing (NLP), tokenization is crucial. It helps convert unprocessed text into machine-understandable tokens. Large Language Models (LLMs) such as GPT, BERT, and T5 are particularly affected by this. This chapter examines the significance of tokenization for LLMs. It shapes how well these models perform tasks such as translation, sentiment analysis, and summarization. This chapter discusses different ways to tokenize text, including word-level, character-level, and subword-level tokenization. Each method has its pros and cons. Subword tokenization methods will also be explored in detail. These include byte-pair encoding (BPE), WordPiece, and the Unigram Language Model. These methods help us handle tricky issues, such as words that are not in the model's vocabulary. This chapter covers various tokenization techniques, including word-level, character-level, and subword-level tokenization, highlighting their respective advantages and limitations. It also explores practical tools, such as Hugging Face tokenizers, and addresses the challenges involved in tokenizing languages with limited resources. Additionally, the chapter examines the critical balance between efficiency, cost, and linguistic richness when selecting the optimal tokenization strategy for different NLP tasks.

Keywords: Byte-Pair Encoding (BPE), Large Language Models (LLMs), Natural Language Processing (NLP), Out-of-Vocabulary (OOV) Words, Subword tokenization, Tokenization.

INTRODUCTION

Tokenization is a very important initial step in the processing pipeline for raw text in Natural Language Processing (NLP), converting it into a form that can be understood by machine learning models, namely large language models running in the background. This includes famous architectures like GPT and BERT/T5: These models were ever made only to read and generate human sentences. Yet, before they can operate on text, it must be divided into smaller components called tokens [1]. Tokenization is one of those layers of abstraction that is much more than splitting at spaces or punctuation; there are sophisticated techniques that will affect the model's ability to capture the nuances of language, the diversity of vocabulary, and the computational complexity.

Sumit Tripathi

The focus of this chapter will be highly specific to LLMs, namely the concept of tokenization, what strategies can be used to tokenize text data into something useful, the challenges of tokenization, and how this is done within state-of-the-art NLP frameworks (Hugging Face). We will also discuss some specific algorithms like byte-pair encoding (BPE), WordPiece, and Unigram Language Model, focusing on their importance in the tokenization step in LLMs. This will enable you to appreciate the value of tokenization, understand the compromises made in different methods, and recognize how it is used in current NLP applications by the end of this chapter.

WHAT IS THE IMPORTANCE OF TOKENIZATION IN A LARGE LANGUAGE MODEL

Tokenization refers to splitting a large corpus of text into smaller units called tokens (words, characters or sub-words). These tokens are then converted to numerical representations that a model can understand. Tokenization is a crucial process that shapes how LLMs understand text, learn patterns, and generate language. To understand why tokenization in LLMs is so important, let's examine its impact across different language processing tasks. Good tokenization retains the context and meaning of the text, and it is essential for performing tasks like translation, summarization, and sentiment analysis [2]. Tokenization, for example, breaks a sentence down into its words rather than its characters, allowing the model to learn grammatical constructs such as what it means for a word to be an adjective and how to understand contextual relationships between words.

Another important aspect of tokenization is its role in handling out-of-vocabulary (OOV) words. For older NLP models, out-of-vocabulary words were a big problem since the model had no way of knowing what these words were. The SentencePiece tokenization method can help with this, as it allows words to be broken down into smaller components. Tokenization is also an important aspect of LLMs' performance. The size of the token sequence produced for a piece of text is directly related to the model's computational cost. The memory and processing power needed for longer sequences can be a limiting factor when scaling to large applications. The most efficient tokenization strategy is one that shortens the sequence length while maintaining as much linguistic information as possible.

But tokenization has its own set of challenges; there is such a thing as a free lunch. The various languages, scripts, syntactic structures, and grammar make it really hard to come up with a tokenization strategy that works across the board. For instance, some languages (like Chinese and Japanese) do not use spaces to separate words, making word-level tokenization more complex. Moreover, the uncertainty of language — where a single word can carry different meanings depending on its context — makes tokenization an even more complex challenge. Tokenization is one of the core processes in LLMs, impacting everything from the model's ability to understand and generate the language to its computational efficiency. The tokenization strategy you choose can have a major effect on your model's performance, making it one of the important factors you should consider when building your NLP systems [3].

TYPES OF TOKENIZATION

Tokenization can be divided into three types: word-level tokenization, character-level tokenization, and subword-level tokenization. So, the methods are compared here by various parameters and ultimately it depends upon the problem statement, *i.e.*, which of them is pushed further in the upcoming version of NLP.

Word-level Tokenization

The most intuitive and well-known approach to tokenization is the word-level tokenization. This method splits text at spaces and punctuation, extracting all words from a block of text. Tokenization: the process of converting words into tokens (tiny text pieces). The sentence "Tokenization is crucial for NLP" will be tokenized as ["Tokenization", "is", "crucial", "for", "NLP"].

The simplicity is one of the main benefits of using word-level tokenization. This aligns with how humans readily parse text, making it easy to encode and interpret. And it works well for English or similar languages, where word boundaries can be easily identified. But, tokenization at the word level is not without its limitations. Dealing with out-of-vocabulary (OOV) words is one of the most challenging issues. Traditional word-level tokenization uses a fixed vocabulary, so if a word doesn't belong to it, it will be marked as unknown. This problem becomes acute in languages with rich morphology, where a single word can take many different forms through inflection, compounding, or derivation. However, the words "run," "running," and "runner," for instance, have the same root but may be treated as completely separate tokens in a word-level tokenization scheme.

Word-level tokenization also restricts the use of space-delimited methods across languages. For example, in Chinese, Japanese, and Thai, there are no spaces between words, which can make it challenging to define what a word is. Character-level tokenization, however, can handle these use cases as they will play well in NLP tasks as well. Although such challenges exist, word-level tokenization is still a method widely used in NLP, especially for types of languages such as English — the method is effective due to its simplicity and natural language aspect.

Character-level Tokenization

An alternative method called character-level tokenization, instead, treats every single character present in the text as an individual token. In the above, the string "Tokenization" will be converted into tokenized words ["T", "o", "k", "e", "n", "i", "z", "a", "t", "i", "o", "n"]. This technique is very instance-specific and language-agnostic, making it suitable for any text instance, irrespective of language or script type. The character-based tokenization is useful for languages that don't separate words with space characters or for those that have more complex writing systems like Arabic or Devanagari. It can also deal with misspellings, slang, or any other unorthodox text that might confuse word-level tokenizers [4].

On the other hand, char-level tokenization may have several shortcomings. A major downside is how long the token sequences it produces can be. Due to the tokenization process, where each character is a token (*i.e.*, breaking a sentence into one token), even a moderately short sentence could yield a long token series. In this way, the text "Tokenization is crucial for NLP" would be tokenized into 28 tokens. With longer token sequences, processing the text requires more computational resources because the model needs to process more tokens, which takes more memory and time.

Models may struggle to learn long-range dependencies and contextual meaning due to another concern with character-level tokenization. Because the model only sees individual characters, it has to learn how to put together context, words, and sentences from these basic units, which is difficult. However, this also means that the models will need much more data and training time to achieve the same performance as with word-level or subword-level tokenization. That said, character-level tokenization is useful for certain situations, such as processing text in languages that lack explicit word boundaries (*e.g.*, Chinese) and for processing text with much variability, such as social media posts, that include misspellings, acronyms, *etc.*

Subword-level Tokenization

Subword Level Tokenization: It is a balance between word-level and character-level tokenization. This approach involves breaking words into smaller units, called subwords. These subwords would typically be common prefixes/suffixes or roots that appear frequently in the text together, as well as common sequences of characters. So, for instance, the word "unhappiness" might be broken down into the tokens ["un", "happi", "ness"]. The main benefit of subword-level tokenization is its better handling of OOV words. Subword tokenization can represent previously unseen words by breaking words into smaller units. For example, it does learn a word representation for "unhappiness," even if it was never in the training data, because it can understand "un" + "happi" + "ness", which might have been seen individually.

This is especially important for morphologically rich languages, where there can be many different word forms. This enables better handling of inflection, derivation, and compounding, as the model can generalize over the parts of a word rather than treating the entire word as a unique token. The other benefit of subword tokenization is efficiency. Subword tokenization methods find a trade-off between capturing linguistic information and maintaining computational efficiency by balancing vocabulary size and language coverage with the length of token sequences. This lends it particularly well to large-scale NLP applications, where processing speed is important.

However, subword tokenization is more complicated than simple word-word or character tokenization. This needs to be carefully tuned so that the generated subwords are useful and actually help with specific NLP task. In addition, although subword tokenization alleviates the OOV issue, it may still not fully capture all the subtleties of language, such as words with meanings beyond their literal meanings or words with meanings bound to form or context.

Note that subword-level tokenization is indeed a very effective and flexible method that overcomes many of the limitations of traditional word- and character-level tokenization methods. Vocabularies are common elements across many NLU tasks, especially when memory limits are reasonable; typically, LLMs are pre-trained on the entire vocabulary and adapt to these general vocabularies during task-based evaluation (short-range). It is important to use universal speech representation to be effective in dealing with OOV words, high-morphologica--richness languages, and large-scale NLP tasks. Notice that this is very common in modern LLMs.

Subword Tokenization in Depth

Subword tokenization is a key technique for modern NLP, notably in the context of LLMs. Such a tokenization feature provides a balance between fine-grained tokenization (which can be achieved at the character level) and the efficiency of word-level tokenization, making it a versatile and effective method for handling diverse text inputs.

Subword Tokenization — Motivation

The main goal of subword tokenization is to address the drawbacks of the word-level or character-level tokenization while also taking advantage of both. Subword tokenization is mostly used to solve the problem of the following challenges:

- **Dealing with Rare and OOV Words:** Dealing with rare words and words not found in the training set is a key issue in NLP. However, typical word-level tokenization does not handle this well, as it can only interpret words in the model's vocabulary. Here is how this challenge is overcome by subword tokenization, which further segments words into smaller units, enabling the model to build unfamiliar words from known subwords.
- **Generalizing Across Forms of a Word:** Many languages, including English, have complex morphological structures where words have a number of forms as a result of inflection, derivation, or compounding. Subword tokenization breaks words into smaller chunks, which helps models generalize across these forms. Tokenization means splitting text into units or chunks, which, in a word-based tokenization, need not mean splitting on a whitespace.
- **Efficiency:** Compared to character-level tokenization, subword tokenization can better balance efficiency and effectiveness, as it balances vocabulary size and the ability to retain useful linguistic information. Subword tokenization enables this by generating fewer tokens per text, resulting in a reduced compute load on the model and expediting its processing and memory consumption.

Subword tokenization is not merely coarse enough to fully express the words in the training set as divisions, without excess vocabulary, to find a trade-off between the average length of token sequences and the vocabulary richness. This balance is essential for providing the efficiency to parse text while also accurately representing words' meaning.

Subword Tokenization Algorithms

Subword tokenization algorithms with various methods of tokenizing the text into a vocabulary to interpret the unknown word. Byte-pair encoding (BPE), WordPiece, and the Unigram Language Model are amongst the most popular algorithms.

Byte-pair Encoding (BPE)

Among the various word tokenization algorithms widely used in contemporary NLP, byte-pair encoding (BPE) has emerged as one of the most favoured choices.

BPE was originally designed for data compression but was repurposed for NLP to produce a small, dense vocabulary [5]. BPE begins with a vocabulary consisting of individual characters and iteratively combines the most frequently occurring pairs of characters (or subwords) into larger subwords. As an example, for the word “happiness”, pairs such as (“h”, “a”), (“a”, “p”), and so on would be merged in subsequent steps until the whole word is represented as one or a few tokens/subwords.

This process is repeated for the most frequent character pairs until a certain vocabulary size is achieved. As a result, the model can achieve very high performance with a limited vocabulary size. This allows for a significant reduction in vocabulary size whilst still preserving a high level of linguistic detail, making BPE particularly powerful. This can be advantageous in models such as GPT-2 with a more compact vocabulary and the complexity to manage simple text formats over one output.

But BPE does have its limitations. This means that pairs of characters that co-occur are merged based solely on their frequency of occurrence, not on meaning. At times, this may lead to suboptimal tokenization—the combination of subwords may not yield linguistically meaningful units. Moreover, BPE lacks the ability to reason in the context in which subwords emerged, leading to ambiguity in the tokenization process. However, BPE suffers from the objection of producing fixed-size vocabulary macros that lack significant linguistic meaning, and it can ignore potentially useful information by failing to capture some of the relevant information encoded in the original corpus.

WordPiece

WordPiece, another subword tokenization algorithm, was introduced in Google's BERT model. Similar to BPE, WordPiece is also a subword model, but unlike BPE, it uses a probabilistic approach to tokenization, maximizing the likelihood of the input sequence. In WordPiece, we start with a vocabulary of characters and iteratively merge subwords based on how likely they are to occur in a probabilistic model. This enables WordPiece to generate subwords that preserve a greater degree of semantic relevance and textual cohesion than alternatives. A major advantage of WordPiece is its robustness to out-of-vocabulary (OOV) words. By decomposing each word into its constituent subwords, WordPiece can provide a meaningful representation even for rare or unseen words. This is especially useful for models like BERT, where accurately representing the nuanced meaning of the text is important, such as in question answering and sentiment analysis tasks [6].

Nonetheless, it's worth noting that WordPiece has a probabilistic nature, which can make tokenization and processing more complex. It can be computationally expensive because the model needs to learn the probabilities of different subwords and their combinations. Word Piece, like BPE, is not context aware, which might yield suboptimal tokenization in certain situations. Yet, despite the complexities involved in creating subword tokens, WordPiece remains an exceptionally robust and adaptable algorithm, and it forms the basis of most other popular NLP models, notably the ones that require a nuanced understanding of semantic elements.

Unigram Language Model

The Unigram Language Model is a subword tokenization algorithm that is less strict than Byte Pair Encoding, as evidenced by its use in models such as SentencePiece. The Unigram Language Model is not a merge-based approach like BPE or WordPiece, but rather a probabilistic model that selects subwords based on their probabilities [7]. The Unigram model begins with a broad vocabulary of potential subwords and progressively eliminates those with low probabilities, determined by how likely the input sequence is. This iterative procedure yields an efficiently represented vocabulary of the training set that is smaller and optimized. The Unigram Language Model has one key advantage, which is its flexibility. It enables different tokenization of the same word, which gives better coverage of the different applied contexts. Such flexibility allows the Unigram model to perform particularly well in applications that require generalization across different languages and types of text, where a single model may not be applicable.

This complexity can lead the Unigram model to have a higher computational cost and take longer to train than simpler models like BPE. The Unigrams model can also, in some potential circumstances, segment words too much, reducing their meaning into meaningless components (tokens). Nonetheless, the Unigram Language Model stands as an effective and adaptable tokenization algorithm that is ideal for state-of-the-art NLP challenges, especially those that need an extensive level of customization and adjustment.

TRADE-OFFS IN TOKENIZATION

There are trade-offs with every tokenization strategy, and the choice of tokenization method is heavily influenced by factors such as the language, the type of model being used, and the specific NLP task. This section is about the - offs in different tokenization strategies, especially from an efficiency-versu- -linguistic richness standpoint.

Tokenization: Word-level *vs.* Character-level

Although word-level tokenization is easy and fast, many tasks in NLP use it. But, it is not quite capable of handling the OOV words, and it is not as flexible in case of the languages that do not have word boundaries. In contrast, character-level tokenization is very flexible and can be applied in a language-independent manner, but it creates long token sequences, raising computational expenses and complicating context capture for models.

Whether to tokenize at the word level or at the character level is largely dependent on the specific nature of the NLP task. On the other hand, for tasks where a deep understanding of language and context is important — such as sentiment analysis or machine translation — it may be more effective to tokenize at the word level. On the other hand, for tasks involving multilingual text or highly diverse textual input, character-based tokenization may prove to be more suitable.

Trade-offs of Subword Tokenization

Subword tokenization strikes a balance between word-level and character-level tokenization, but it comes with its own trade-offs. One of the primary trade-offs is vocabulary size versus sequence length. Unlike byte pair encoding, which results in shorter subword tokens that capture meaning as compared to standard word levels, and thus lower vocabulary size, this can lead to longer token sequences. This trade-off is of critical importance in large scale NLP applications, where efficiency in processing is paramount. A second trade-off is between efficiency and contextual understanding in subword tokenization. Although subword tokenization is usually more efficient than tokenization at the character level, it can still miss some context-specific details, especially in languages that have a complex morphology. On the other end are languages like Finnish: words can take 200 or more forms, so subword tokenization doesn't always let you understand what that particular token means in that context.

Also, BPE and WordPiece are simple and easy to implement subword tokenization algorithms, but they have the possibility to generate not very good tokens in certain cases. At the same time, sophisticated algorithms such as Unigram Language Model have the advantage of flexibility and adaptability at the cost of increased computational requirements and tuning effort. There are trade-offs between efficiency, linguistic richness, and contextual understanding in the choice of a tokenization strategy. The best tokenization method varies depending on the NLP task, target language, and resources used.

TOKENIZATION IN PRACTICE — HUGGING FACE TOKENIZERS

Hugging Face has quickly emerged as one of the leading figures in the NLP community, thanks to its extraordinarily extensive collection of models and tools that make a variety of NLP tasks simple to implement. This extensive support for tokenization techniques is essential since it offers pre-processed text data that is appropriate for a machine learning model. The act of tokenizing text involves breaking it up into smaller chunks, such as words or subwords, so that a model can comprehend and process it efficiently. With the use of the Hugging Face library's highly effective and adaptable tokenizers, users can customize tokenization to meet particular tasks and dataset requirements.

Hugging Face Tokenizers

The Hugging Face tokenizers are very efficient and flexible, letting users preprocess text data as needed for their specific application. It supports the following tokenization methods:

- **BPE Tokenizer:** An efficient tokenizer that acts as an optimizer using Byte-Pair Encoding to minimize the vocabulary size. It is a pure tokenized model with a rich understanding of text with a large vocabulary.
- **WordPiece Tokenizer:** Commonly used in models such as BERT; this tokenizer offers powerful tokenization that optimizes the trade-off between vocabulary size and sequence length. It's especially powerful for tasks such as question answering and sentiment analysis, which almost require deep semantic understanding.
- **Increased tokenization flexibility and compactness using the Unigram LM:** SentencePiece Tokenizer is optimal for multilingual models and translation tasks and for use cases with a significant amount of specific behavior expected from the model.
- Hugging Face tokenizers are highly customizable, allowing users to adjust parameters such as vocabulary size, special tokens (*e.g.*, [CLS], [SEP]), and how to handle unknown tokens. This flexibility allows Hugging Face tokenizers to be used in a variety of NLP tasks, such as text classification and machine translation.

Customizing Tokenization

Custom Article: One of the best features of Hugging Face tokenizers is their high level of customization. This allows users to customize the tokenization process to meet their particular needs and make adjustments for parameters such as:

- **Restriction of Vocabulary:** Users can set the vocabulary size, which would act as a trade-off between the length of the input sequence and verisimilitude. Using fewer vocabulary tokens leads to shorter sequences (reducing computational costs) but can also cause loss of information regarding the nuance of the text, while more tokens in the vocabulary lead to richer detail but increase computational costs.
- **Special Tokens**: Hugging Face tokenizers let users create special tokens for tasks such as classification or sequence-to-sequence modelling. So, the [CLS] token can be used to predict the entire sequence in a classification task, and the [SEP] token can separate different segments in a single input.
- **Handling Unseen Tokens:** Users can define handling for unseen tokens (*i.e.*, tokens not in the vocabulary). Such unknown tokens can be replaced by a special [UNK] token or broken apart into smaller pieces, called subwords.

This degree of customization and control means that Hugging Face tokenizers can be used for a wide variety of NLP tasks, in research and production.

Tokenization and Its Integration with Models

Hugging Face tokenizers work out of the box with pre-trained models on the Hugging Face Model Hub. By combining these two open-source tools, it becomes straightforward to tokenize data, as well as train models, allowing users to harness the power of cutting-edge NLP techniques without extensive effort. The pre-trained BERT needs to be matched with the text preprocessing using the appropriate WordPiece tokenizer after being downloaded from the Hugging Face Model Hub. Through the use of specific tokens, padding, and truncation, tokenization automatically transforms the text into the necessary format. The workflow in NLP is streamlined by this smooth integration of tokenization with the model, freeing users from managing the complexities of tokenization techniques to concentrate on fine-tuning and optimizing the models. This method greatly improves the NLP pipeline's usability and efficiency.

MULTILINGUAL AND LOW-RESOURCE TOKENIZATION CHALLENGES

Tokenization has especially become challenging for multilingual and low-resource languages. This means that standard tokenization strategies may not be enough, and so, these kinds of problems may need more sophisticated approaches.

Multilingual Tokenization

Tokenization in multilingual models is more complex because the way letters or words are combined into tokens differs across languages. These setups commonly use subword tokenization, a language-agnostic method for segmenting words into smaller units. In multilingual models, one common approach is to use a shared vocabulary and share the subwords across languages. This reduces the model's overall vocabulary size, but results in suboptimal tokenization for certain languages. Common subwords in one language might not make sense in some other language, resulting in this potential ambiguity and inaccuracy.

To solve these challenges, some multilingual models apply separate tokenizers for each language, enabling more language-specific tokenization. This increases the model's complexity but may improve the accuracy of tokenization required for each language. Writing systems and scripts are another area of challenge for multilingual tokenization. Latin-based languages such as English and Spanish do use spaces between words, but others, such as Chinese and Japanese do not. This diversity makes it challenging to create a one-size-fits-all tokenization strategy for all languages. Multilingual tokenization is an important topic of current research and development, despite these challenges, as it enables the creation of models that can handle and comprehend multiple languages within a single architecture.

Low-resource Languages: Tokenization

Tokenization can also be particularly challenging for low-resource languages, which have little training data. Applied this way, the model can struggle to learn what tokenization strategy is best with moulded data. Data augmentation is one way to overcome this, that is, artificially increasing the amount of training data available to the system by creating new instances from the existing instances. As an illustration, adding training examples *via* data augmentation techniques that translate the text into a different language and back to the original language (back-translation), or generate paraphrases that replace each word in a text with a new word (paraphrase), *etc.* Another direction is transfer learning, in which knowledge from high-resource languages is transferred to low-resource languages. With this, you can pre-train a model on a large corpus of high-resource language data, and then fine-tune it on less data for low-resource languages. Transfer learning can improve tokenization and general model performance in low-resource scenarios by leveraging similarities across languages.

Furthermore, MT for low-resource languages could be improved through multilingual models that leverage a shared vocabulary spanning languages, as this would enable low-resource languages to benefit from training on data from related high-resource languages. In low-resource languages, tokenization remains a complex and active area of ongoing research, and new methods, such as data augmentation and transfer learning, continue to push the boundaries in this more challenging space [8].

TOKENIZATION IN MODERN LARGE LANGUAGE MODELS

Modern LLMs like CPT, BERT, and T5 rely heavily on tokenization strategies in their design and implementation. All these models come with their own tokenization methods, which affect model performance and generalization.

Tokenization in GPT

The GPT (Generative Pre-trained Transformer) model employs byte-pair encoding (BPE) for its tokenization. Byte Pair Encoding (BPE) is an algorithm for subword tokenization that starts with characters and unsupervisedly merges the most frequently occurring character pairs (or subwords) to minimize vocabulary size. As a result of this simple operation, GPT can achieve a general approach to completing text input across different datasets with a relatively small vocabulary, making unified operation highly efficient and effective for handling large-scale NLP tasks.

The most significant benefit of the BPE in GPT usage is its advantage of dividing rare words and out-of-vocabulary (OOV) words into subwords. Then, by further breaking the words into subword tokens (for example, the word "unhappiness" gets tokenized as ["un", "happi", "ness"]), the model can still get a good representation of the words and its context (just that either of the subword tokens may have not been present in the training dataset). But BPE merges only based on frequency, which can lead to suboptimal tokenization in some cases. More specifically, BPE may combine character(s) and/or subword(s) that are common co-occurrences but do not correspond to meaningful linguistic units. Arabic and Hindi words, for example, can become ambiguous when tokenized using BPE, as it does not consider context when growing subwords.

Overall, BPE strikes a balance between splitting tokens at linguistic boundaries and being efficient in terms of space, and is therefore an effective choice as a tokenization algorithm for GPT. It has remained a staple for constructing rich representations in more recent LLMs despite these limitations.

Tokenization in BERT

BERT (Bidirectional Encoder Representations from Transformers); however, uses WordPiece tokenizer, which is optimized for generating semantically meaningful tokens. WordPiece builds on BPE, but with a probabilistic tokenization model that maximizes the probability of the input sequence. By breaking down the text in a more linguistically appropriate manner so as to form little subword chunks such that the meaning of the text is captured more holistically, the BERT tokenizer is therefore capable of representing semantics in a manner less tied to the vocabulary of the corpus. A common tokenization strategy is to break words into subwords, allowing the model to learn composite words; for instance, the word "unhappiness" could be tokenized into ["un", "happiness"] so the model understands that "un-" and "happiness" each have meanings and are meaningful units.

The WordPiece tokenizer is mainly beneficial due to its robustness to OOV words. Wordpiece solves this by splitting words into smaller subwords, allowing it to build a culturally meaningful representation of even the rarest or unseen words. This enables it to perform very well on tasks such as question answering and sentiment analysis, where understanding the subtle meaning of text is crucial." In contrast, the WordPiece's probabilistic approach makes tokenization a more complex process. This means the model needs to learn the probabilities of different subwords and their combinations, which can be computationally intensive. However, like BPE, WordPiece does not fully exploit the context in which subwords appear, which may yield less-than-ideal tokenization in some cases. Nevertheless, the WordPiece tokenizer is a very powerful and efficient subword tokenization algorithm that has been successfully adopted in many state-of-the-art NLP models, particularly for tasks that demand high semantic understanding.

Tokenization in T5

T5 (Text-to-Text Transfer Transformer) implements a SentencePiece tokenizer using the Unigram Language Model. Whereas both BPE and WordPiece are merging-based, the Unigram Language Model chooses subwords based on the likelihood of a subword within a probabilistic model. T5 SentencePiece tokenizer is capable of a coverage approach in terms of text input with a small vocabulary. Such flexibility makes T5 especially well-suited for tasks that require high adaptability and even customization, such as text generation and translation. An important feature of the SentencePiece tokenizer is a multi-lingual and cross-script (one model for multiple languages/scripts) tokenizer. SentencePiece, built on the Unigram Language Model, can form a shared vocabulary root across languages, enabling T5 to process multilingual text in its inputs. On the other hand, the Unigram Language Model's complexity can also result in over-segmentation; in this case, words are divided into subwords that do not carry any semantic meaning. Moreover, there are cases where the characteristics of the Unigram model can lead to the loss of meaning or context.

CONCLUSION

The importance of tokenization for the performance of Large Language Models (LLMs) is emphasized in the chapter's conclusion. LLMs can process and generate text efficiently while preserving the linguistic structures and meanings required for correct outputs through efficient tokenization. Word-level tokenization offers a straightforward approach but encounters challenges with out-of-vocabulary (OOV) words and languages that lack clear word boundaries. Character-level tokenization offers greater flexibility but results in longer token sequences, which increase computational demands. Modern NLP tasks benefit from subword-level tokenization methods such as byte-pair encoding (BPE), WordPiece, and the Unigram Language Model, as they strike an optimal balance between processing speed and linguistic complexity. The chapter underscores the necessity of choosing tokenization methods by examining trade-offs among strategies while considering task demands, linguistic structures, and computational limitations. The ongoing development of tokenization methods, combined with models like GPT, BERT, and T5, will boost multilingual and text variety processing capabilities, enhancing LLM performance in practical applications.

REFERENCES

[1] N. Rajaraman, J. Jiao, and K. Ramchandran, "Toward a theory of tokenization in LLMs", Apr. 12, 2024.
[http://dx.doi.org/10.48550/arXiv.2404.08335]

[2] Z. Li, and X. Lu, "Research on compressed input sequences based on compiler tokenization", *Information (Basel),* vol. 16, no. 2, p. 73, 2025.
[http://dx.doi.org/10.3390/info16020073]

[3] R. Sennrich, B. Haddow, and A. Birch, "Neural machine translation of rare words with subword units," in *Proceedings of the 54th Annual Meeting of the Association for Computational Linguistics (Volume 1: Long Papers)*, K. Erk and N. A. Smith, Eds. Berlin, Germany: Association for Computational Linguistics, 2016, pp. 1715–1725.
[http://dx.doi.org/10.18653/v1/P16-1162]

[4] A. Morales-Pastor, "Character-level tokenizations as powerful inductive biases for RNA foundational models", Nov. 05, 2024.
[http://dx.doi.org/10.48550/arXiv.2411.11808]

[5] V. Zouhar, "A formal perspective on byte-pair encoding", Sep. 02, 2024.
[http://dx.doi.org/10.48550/arXiv.2306.16837]

[6] X. Song, A. Salcianu, Y. Song, D. Dopson, and D. Zhou, "Fast wordpiece tokenization", In:

Proceedings of the 2021 Conference on Empirical Methods in Natural Language Processing (EMNLP 2021) Association for Computational Linguistics: Punta Cana, Dominican Republic, 2021, pp. 2089-2103.
[http://dx.doi.org/10.18653/v1/2021.emnlp-main.160]

[7] J. Roh, S-H. Oh, and S-Y. Lee, "Unigram-normalized perplexity as a language model performance measure with different vocabulary sizes", Nov. 26, 2020.
[http://dx.doi.org/10.48550/arXiv.2011.13220]

[8] Y. Wu, "Google's neural machine translation system: bridging the gap between human and machine translation", Oct. 08, 2016.
[http://dx.doi.org/10.48550/arXiv.1609.08144]

CHAPTER 4

The Association of the System with the Prompt

Abstract: In the framework of Large Language Models (LLMs), the chapter explores the importance of prompts in promoting successful human-machine interactions. It describes prompts as user inputs intended to elicit particular replies from AI systems, identifying them as fundamental components of human-machine communication. Prompt dynamics over time are thoroughly examined, covering both their immediate and long-term impacts on model behavior. The conversation emphasizes how precise versus open-ended cues affect interaction patterns and promote user involvement. Analysis of the function of memory and context in prompting shows how past encounters influence present and future interactions, enabling more individualized and cohesive conversations. In order to maximize human-machine interactions, useful suggestions for creating powerful prompts are also offered, highlighting the significance of precision, clarity, and engagement. Prompt construction's ethical aspects are thoroughly investigated, paying particular attention to issues of privacy, bias, and inclusion. In this chapter, the potential future of prompt-driven interactions is examined, along with their revolutionary uses in industries including customer service, healthcare, and education. It highlights how important ethical design principles are to making sure AI systems function in an inclusive and responsible manner while encouraging innovation in a variety of sectors.

Keywords: Ethical AI design, Human-machine interaction, Large Language Models (LLMs), Memory and context, Prompt engineering, Prompt dynamics.

INTRODUCTION

Prompts are the primary means of human-machine interaction, providing the necessary context to construct a conversation with a large language model (LLM). In this chapter, the notion of prompts is introduced in all its hcadachc-causing forms, its temporal situatedness, its existence as user input, and its relation to memory and context. Definition of a Prompt: In human-computer interaction and natural language processing, a prompt is a stimulus or cue — generally given to a large language model (LLM) or other AI-powered interface — to elicit a response. It is a command or input, given by a user or a system, to generate an output, mostly text but also any type of media. Any prompt is also used, referring to a prompt that takes the form of a question, a command, a request, or a

Sumit Tripathi

statement, designed to stimulate a response in the form of wanted information or action from the system. This helps establish the purpose or guidelines for the system to follow in order to understand the user's intent and produce an appropriate and contextually relevant response. Prompts are the key element that establishes interaction with LLMs or other AI systems, as we need to provide prompts to get a conversation going. They allow users to express their needs, preferences, and questions in natural language, making it possible to use them for a variety of tasks, from information retrieval to completing tasks, and decision-making to creativity [1].

Designing effective prompts requires careful attention to aspects like clarity, specificity, relevance, and user engagement. Clear, well-structured prompts guide users to ask better queries, while more specific prompts enable the system to craft more accurate, appropriate answers. Relevant prompts are those that align with the user's objectives and desired outcomes, ensuring that any generated output fulfils specific needs and requirements. With these factors in mind, you can create prompts that not only invite users to make inquiries but also set the stage for an engaging conversation that creates a more memorable experience. Prompts are the mechanisms through which users and systems communicate: whether this be a user asking a question and the system responding, or a system generating prompts based on prescribed algorithms, models, or training systems [2]. Prompt performance is determined by what you enter, the model, and the context in which and when a prompt is given. In summary, a user prompt is the basic building block of human-machine communication, ensuring users can communicate meaningfully and efficiently with AI systems. The process of receiving input in response to a prompt and providing suitable output is crucial for developing effective systems for these types of user interactions. Prompt engineering: We present the supporting techniques in Fig. (**1**).

TEMPORAL DIMENSION OF PROMPTS

The temporal dimension of prompt dynamics encompasses both simultaneous and time-dependent effects on interactions between the prompt and the LLM [3]. So, for example, a user question *"What is the capital of France?"* elicits an immediate answer from the LLM based on what it knows and gets the answer *"Paris"*. For example, long-term prompts only tell the model how to respond during future interactions; if you want to affect the behaviour of the model over time through multiple interactions, you can do so using long-term prompts. Example: A single user who always gives prompts on cooking recipes. It takes several prompts to learn from during interactive sessions, and gradually adjusts its responses, offering increasingly accurate and helpful cooking guidance. This is an example of how long-term prompts can shape a model's behaviour and responsivity over time. The dynamics of how immediate and long-term prompt effects interact highlight the nature of these interactions with LLMs. It is crucial to understand this temporal context if we want to exploit the far-reaching potential of prompt dynamics, both for fetching up-to-date data and for controlling the model's behaviour during longer engagements.

To demonstrate the temporal dimension of prompts, consider the following hypothetical dialogue between a user and an LLM:

Outcome:

User: *"How's the weather looking tomorrow?"*

Large Language Model: *"Tomorrow's weather forecast indicates sunshine and a high of 75°F."*

Here, the user prompt leads to a real-time interaction with the LLM, delivering the current weather prediction.

User: *"Starting now, when I inquire about the weather, give me a detailed report for the next three days."*

LLM: *"Understood. I will use your preference in my subsequent responses."*

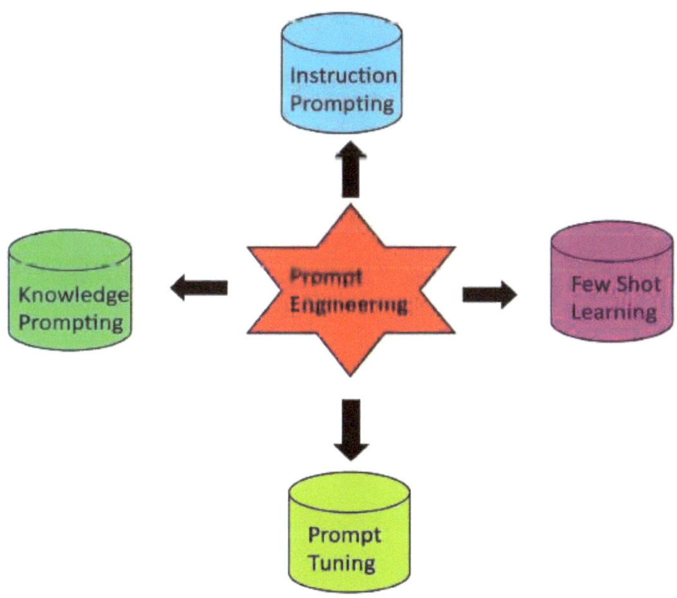

Fig. (1). Associated methods/prompts.

Here, the user's actions act as a long-term prompt: each interaction would tell the LLM to change its subsequent behaviour, and, with this, give detailed weather predictions over the course of several days.

Investigating both short- and long-term consequences provides insight into how prompts govern engagement with LLMs, shaping the nature of human-MLM dialogue.

PROMPTING USER INPUT

Prompts serve as valuable triggers for user interaction, encouraging engagement and directing conversations around specific topics. They come in many forms, ranging from wide-open questions to specific commands, all designed to get users to be creative and deliver useful information. Open-ended prompts encourage users to express their thoughts, opinions, or experiences, fostering a broader, more fluid exchange [4], however, given that general instructions direct users to provide concrete details, helping the discussion stay on task toward the set goals. This is because the real challenge about prompting is that it has two distinct purposes: an invitation to user participation and the influence of a conversation to form the information that can be shared in a meaningful way.

Consider a user who needs information about a topic:

User: *“Explain the history of artificial intelligence.”*

LLM: *“Artificial intelligence, or AI, is a branch of computer science...”*

Here, the user’s prompt signals that LLM is required to generate a lengthy, holistic response, explaining the history of artificial intelligence.

The second important element for eliciting user input is prompting for clarification, which enables the user to refine their query or give overall context. For instance:

User: *“I want to learn about AI ethics. Do you have any resources that can help?”*

LLM: *“Certainly! “Yes, could you clarify the areas of AI ethics you’re most interested in?”*

Here, the LLM asks the user clarifying questions, requesting more specificity to personalize its reply.

In addition, you can prompt them to engage with the discussion, allowing for two-way communication and increased interaction. This approach helps LLM to generate more personalized and meaningful responses, as users are encouraged to share their opinions, experiences, or preferences by being asked to because of this prompt.

To show how prompts help elicit user input, what about a conversation like this:

User: *"What are the best restaurants in New York City?"*

LLM: *"New York City is home to many great restaurants, some of which include:.."*

The user prompt starts a back-and-forth discussion with the LLM about restaurant recommendations, and the LLM responds based on its knowledge base.

User: *"I'm a vegetarian. Is there a vegetarian option on the restaurant menu?"*

LLM: *"Of course! "Let me look up some vegetarian options for you."*

In the example shown, the user's prompt asks the LLM to shape its response based on the user's dietary restrictions, inviting the use of prompts relevant to the user.

Prompting effectively creates such conversations with LLMs, and this further leads to better engaging user interaction.

MEMORY AND CONTEXT IN PROMPTS

This interplay between memory and context comes to influence the prompt dynamics, how the responses from the model are influenced by previous interactions, and the context surrounding it. In this context, 'memory' means the model's ability to remember information and integrate that with what you've talked about in previous exchanges [5]. Well-formulated prompts serve as memory cues, prompting the model to access and use pertinent information from its memory reserve. Past conversations help to create a more natural and coherent conversation between the user and the AI model as they provide context from previous exchanges, enabling the model to continue from where it left off and ensuring that the conversation flows without interruption.

Moreover, prompts leverage context to customize responses that meet users' needs and preferences. Contextual factors, including a user's history, location, or prior queries, inform the model's interpretation of the input [6]. These contextual variables guide the model in producing responses that are both relevant and tailored to the individual user. This allows the system to understand the context of the conversation and respond appropriately, making interactions more relevant and useful, as the model's output can adjust to the nuances of the current exchange and the specific traits of the user in question.

Imagine a user who has a conversation with an LLM into a series of conversations:

Example: **User:** *"Can you suggest a good book to read?"*

LLM: *"Sure! An inspired recommendation, based on your previous interest in science fiction..."*

This is an example of memory where the LLM's response is influenced by past interactions with the user (similar to a doctor diagnosing a patient, remembering past ailments and treatments for the same patient) to give better recommendations.

User: *"I have a trip planned to Italy. Any travel tips?"*

LLM: *"Absolutely! Some suggestions based on your upcoming trip to Italy..."*

In this example, the LLM's answer is context-dependent and includes details of the user's planned trip to Italy to offer travel advice and suggestions.

Prompts enable LLMs to provide more personalized and relevant responses by harnessing memory and context, resulting in an improved interaction for both users and the model.

CRAFTING EFFECTIVE PROMPTS

There are numerous factors that determine the effectiveness of prompts, with clarity, specificity, and user engagement among the most crucial. Therefore, prompts must be well-structured and intentional to facilitate the model's best performance and to elicit more meaningful, productive outputs in conversation. Focus on clarity — your prompts should be descriptive enough for users to understand what they should do easily. Clear prompts reduce ambiguity so that users understand what queries or directives are meant. Essentially, such clarity serves as a basis for prompting a model to produce accurate and pertinent responses. Specific prompts guide user interaction toward the information of interest. Clearly structured prompts help users enter detailed, relevant information, allowing the model to produce more precise, context-sensitive replies. These prompts work to keep the interaction efficient and meaningful.

The dynamic interaction of creating prompts that engage the user and get them interested in the material is User Engagement. Such prompts encourage user behaviour that leads to interesting answers, which improves the overall quality of interaction and consequently, the user experience. Understanding how sequence lengths, token counts, and prompt design principles affect model performance helps ensure effective interactions with ChatGPT. Such structured placement of prompts creates an efficient, easily navigable sleuthing process that cultivates the exchange of ideas.

PROMPT STRUCTURING FOR BEST OUTPUT

One of the most fundamental characteristics of effective prompts is clarity and specificity, which help users understand what we want to do or what information we seek from them. Writing prompts in language that is clear, focused, and succinct is the best way to avoid ambiguity and confusion, which can both undermine the user experience in interacting with the software and generate less relevant and accurate replies. Clear prompts are those that communicate their meaning in an unambiguous way, with no room for misunderstanding. It is in this context that the purpose of implementing clear guidelines or instructions becomes essential for steering users to provide the information or take the action anticipated by the system. It encourages a simple and intuitive interaction, making it easy for users to understand the purpose of the prompt without any additional complexity.

Specificity in prompts reduces the attentional area and directs users to click in to give precise, relevant answers. Specific prompts guide users to know the exact information or action needed, instead of leaving room for wide interpretation. It is particularly important in applications where a detailed and contextually relevant input is needed for the system to generate accurate outputs. This approach focuses on interacting clearly and in a well-defined manner — thereby improving how we communicate with the system, reducing any chance of miscommunication, and increasing the effectiveness of the interaction. Most likely, clear prompts foster output when the input is succinct, simple, and specific, encouraging a positive, efficient user experience.

Here are a few examples of prompts you could submit:

User: *"Tell me about climate change?"*

LLM: *"Certainly! The following is a roundup of important facts and figures on climate change..."*

For example, the user in the above case is asking a clear question about climate change, which requires LLM to provide information.

User: *"Tell me more about the environment."*

LLM: *"Can you please clarify what aspect of the environment you would like to know more about?"*

This prompt, on the contrary, is ambiguous and non-specific and will need the LLM to ask the user for clarifications before providing a relevant response.

MAXIMIZING PROMPT IMPACT

Thoughtfully crafted prompts are essential in generating detailed and relevant responses from users, creating meaningful interactions, and increasing engagement. Prompts asking open-ended questions, where users are encouraged to share their opinions, experiences, or preferences, are critical to driving rich, informative dialogue. This leads to improvement in the overall experience and depth of engagement between users and the system [7]. Asking users to share opinions or personal points of view does not just ask for information; it invites them to participate in the conversation. Value of Engaging Prompts: Such prompts stimulate interest and curiosity, to systematically offer a more sophisticated and nuanced response. This not only makes for a more dynamic and interactive experience for users, but also yields valuable feedback that can be used to improve the system's understanding of user behaviour and the relevance of its recommendations. Prompts written a way that hit certain personal points, hold them more involved and engaged. Not only does this make the information richer and more contextual, but it also creates a positive user experience, since the interactions become more enjoyable and meaningful.

Some examples of prompts you may try are:

User: *"What do you think about renewable energy?"*

LLM: *"I think renewable energy is key to..."*

For instance, in this example of a prompt given to an LLM, the user is incentivizing the LLM to express its own thoughts and opinions on renewable energy to facilitate conversation.

Prompt: *"Can you provide a summary of recent advancements in renewable energy technologies?"*

LLM: *"Certainly! Here are some highlights of progress..."*

In one such conversation, a user asks for a comprehensive summary of recent developments in renewable energy technologies, highlighting how effective prompts can yield valuable insights and discuss progress in multiple fields.

ETHICS IN PROMPT ENGINEERING

Prompt design must always take ethical considerations into account, ensuring respectful, non-intrusive, and unbiased interactions with large language models (LLMs). Indeed, user privacy and confidentiality become a core principle that needs to be protected during such an interaction process. So, aside from a potential privacy infringement, tackling bias is necessary if we are to bring diverse and fair exchange into Human-Machine Interaction. An ethical approach to prompt design actively combats bias in the outputs produced by LLMs, which helps support inclusivity and avoid harmful stereotypes. By following transparent and inclusive principles of prompt-making, we can reduce the likelihood that LLMs will perpetuate certain biases in their output. Prompt design ethics also extends to avoiding negative prompt mechanisms that could lead to bad-designed interactions that utter nonsense or provoke anger. Through the extension of ethical principles in the design process, we can nurture a responsible and trustworthy environment for human-machine interaction, so that technology properly serves as a beneficial and inclusive tool across applications.

Ethical prompt design considerations include:

- **Honor User Privacy and Confidentiality:** Safeguarding user privacy and confidentiality in prompt design, so that sensitive information is treated and processed securely and ethically.

Examples may include: Mitigating Bias and Promoting Diversity: It may also include the efforts made to mitigate bias and promote diversity in prompt-generated content, encouraging inclusiveness and fairness in the interactions with LLM.

- **Transparency and Accountability**: Standards may establish requirements that the prompt design practices be transparent and accountable, and that users are made aware of grid components and their use to promote informed decisions regarding LLM interactions.

Incorporating ethical considerations into prompt design can help ensure that interactions with LLMs are conducted responsibly and ethically, respecting user rights and promoting positive outcomes for all stakeholders.

APPLICATIONS AND FUTURE DIRECTIONS

Prompts have the potential to impact diverse areas, from education to healthcare to customer service to entertainment. The advancement of human-machine interaction using LLMs continues to show unprecedented potential, from refining current strategies to allowing new forms of interaction with LLMs through prompt-based interactions [8].

Here are examples of prompt-based applications that could be built:

- **Etienne:** Educational Value Large Language Models (LLMs) make for great tutors and, with interactive prompts and conversation, provide rich personalized educational support. Students can chat, throw queries, and get custom-made explanations, which makes the learning rich and interactive.
- **Healthcare Support:** LLMs also provide assistance in healthcare—prompting users through symptoms, medications, and wellness. This enables users to get healthcare assistance and information on various healthcare queries.
- **Customer Service Automation:** LLMs automate customer service interactions, handle inquiries, and provide support through prompt-driven dialogues, improving response efficiency. Such automation makes processes more efficient, allows responding faster, and increases customer satisfaction.
- **Entertainment and Content Generation:** The creativity of LLMs is front and centre, offering entertainment methods and content. Users can engage in storytelling, gaming, and interactive media through prompt-based interactions, generating dynamic, personalized entertainment in response to their input.

Artificial Intelligence systems, also known as AI, have witnessed significant changes and advancements in the past few years, but thus far, as we see the changes, we need to consider the ethics and societal impacts of such systems as we move toward prompt-based systems.

The Future of Prompt-based Interactions

With advancements in AI technology and natural language processing, the future of prompt-based interactions looks very promising. The potential applications for leveraging LLMs to boost productivity, creativity, and collaboration are boundless as researchers and developers continue to optimize prompt strategies and uncover new use cases.

Key takeaway: At the heart of this interaction with any large language model you can build something out of are the prompts that you throw at it; they define the conversation, with the model tailored to you. The manipulation of words can help us optimize the performance of LLMs, making them powerful tools to transform the way we talk, teach, do business, and connect in the age of the Internet. So, if you're ready to dive into the exciting world of Prompt Engineering, join us on this journey to explore the art of talking to machines and how it can redefine our future in unimaginable ways! With the right design, implementation, and conversation, we can better harness the power of prompts and further progress towards a more conscious, smart and human-centric future of human-machine interaction. Step by step, we work on bringing that vision to life— not only of a world where technology enables positive transformations, enriches the lives of our users, and empowers different individuals, but also a world where traversal between borders is facilitated, and connections blossom beyond what used to be possible or common. Here, in taking this first step together, we activate the possibility of prompts to create a future that is connected and generative in ways that ripple through generations.

CONCLUSION

Prompts play a pivotal role in ensuring successful communication between humans and AI, particularly when it comes to large language models (LLMs). Thoughtfully designed prompts are the foundation for obtaining meaningful and impactful responses from these systems. Their structure and clarity significantly shape how well people engage with AI. Both short-term and long-term effects of prompt design are critical, influencing how LLMs respond in real-time or adapt through repeated interactions. By creating prompts that are clear, precise, and engaging, users can improve the relevance and accuracy of AI outputs. Incorporating memory and context into prompt creation further enhances the personalization and coherence of these exchanges. The chapter also underscores the ethical dimensions of prompt engineering, urging the protection of user privacy, the reduction of bias, and the advancement of diversity in AI interactions. As LLMs continue to advance, their applications across various sectors—like education, healthcare, and customer service—are expanding rapidly. With careful attention to how prompts are crafted, we can harness the vast potential of these systems while ensuring their use is responsible, ethical, and beneficial.

REFERENCES

[1] N. Knoth, A. Tolzin, A. Janson, and J.M. Leimeister, "AI literacy and its implications for prompt engineering strategies", *Comput. Aided Eng. Appl.*, vol. 6, p. 100225, 2024. [http://dx.doi.org/10.1016/j.caeai.2024.100225]

[2] L. Wang, R. Song, W. Guo, and H. Yang, "Exploring prompt pattern for generative artificial intelligence in automatic question generation", *Interact. Learn. Environ.*, pp. 1-17, 2024.

[http://dx.doi.org/10.1080/10494820.2024.2412082]

[3] J. Hu, X. Liu, Z. Fan, Y. Yin, S. Xiang, S. Ramasamy, and R. Zimmermann, "Prompt-based spatio-temporal graph transfer learning," in *Proceedings of the 33rd ACM International Conference on Information and Knowledge Management (CIKM '24)*, Boise, ID, USA: *Association for Computing Machinery*, 2024, pp. 890–899. [http://dx.doi.org/10.1145/3627673.3679554]

[4] O. Fagbohun, R.M. Harrison, and A. Dereventsov, "An empirical categorization of prompting techniques for large language models: A practitioner's guide", Feb. 18, 2024. [http://dx.doi.org/10.48550/arXiv.2402.14837]

[5] Y.K. Dwivedi, N. Kshetri, L. Hughes, E.L. Slade, A. Jeyaraj, A.K. Kar, A.M. Baabdullah, A. Koohang, V. Raghavan, M. Ahuja, H. Albanna, M.A. Albashrawi, A.S. Al-Busaidi, J. Balakrishnan, Y. Barlette, S. Basu, I. Bose, L. Brooks, D. Buhalis, L. Carter, S. Chowdhury, T. Crick, S.W. Cunningham, G.H. Davies, R.M. Davison, R. Dé, D. Dennehy, Y. Duan, R. Dubey, R. Dwivedi, J.S. Edwards, C. Flavián, R. Gauld, V. Grover, M-C. Hu, M. Janssen, P. Jones, I. Junglas, S. Khorana, S. Kraus, K.R. Larsen, P. Latreille, S. Laumer, F.T. Malik, A. Mardani, M. Mariani, S. Mithas, E. Mogaji, J.H. Nord, S. O'Connor, F. Okumus, M. Pagani, N. Pandey, S. Papagiannidis, I.O. Pappas, N. Pathak, J. Pries-Heje, R. Raman, N.P. Rana, S-V. Rehm, S. Ribeiro-Navarrete, A. Richter, F. Rowe, S. Sarker, B.C. Stahl, M.K. Tiwari, W. van der Aalst, V. Venkatesh, G. Viglia, M. Wade, P. Walton, J. Wirtz, and R. Wright, "Opinion paper: "So what if ChatGPT wrote it?" Multidisciplinary perspectives on opportunities, challenges and implications of generative conversational AI for research, practice and policy", *Int. J. Inf. Manage.*, vol. 71, 2023. [http://dx.doi.org/10.1016/j.ijinfomgt.2023.102642]

[6] J.Z. Wang, S. Zhao, C. Wu, R.B. Adams, M.G. Newman, T. Shafir, and R. Tsachor, "Unlocking the emotional world of visual media: An overview of the science, research, and impact of understanding emotion", *Proc. IEEE,* vol. 111, no. 10, pp. 1236-1286, 2023. [http://dx.doi.org/10.1109/JPROC.2023.3273517] [PMID: 37859667]

[7] A. Bodonhelyi, E. Bozkir, S. Yang, E. Kasneci, and G. Kasneci, "User intent recognition and satisfaction with large language models: A user study with ChatGPT", Nov. 19, 2024. [http://dx.doi.org/10.48550/arXiv.2402.02136]

[8] K. Shah, A.Y. Xu, Y. Sharma, M. Daher, C. McDonald, B.G. Diebo, and A.H. Daniels, "Large language model prompting techniques for advancement in clinical medicine", *J. Clin. Med.,* vol. 13, no. 17, p. 5101, 2024. [http://dx.doi.org/10.3390/jcm13175101] [PMID: 39274316]

CHAPTER 5

Using Patterns in Personas with Language Models

Abstract: The idea of persona patterns in language models and their revolutionary effects on natural language processing (NLP) are explored in depth in this chapter. These patterns enable language models to adopt different identities, each with unique communication styles, personality traits, and knowledge bases. By leveraging these personas, AI systems can generate contextually appropriate and highly tailored responses, thereby enhancing the effectiveness and engagement of interactions across diverse applications. The chapter highlights how persona patterns can significantly elevate user experiences in fields such as marketing, education, and customer service by aligning responses with the unique needs and expectations of users. It provides a detailed examination of the foundational elements required to design persona patterns, emphasizing the importance of integrating critical domain knowledge, nuanced communication methods, and coherent personality traits to enrich AI interactions. In addition, the chapter addresses the ethical dimensions of persona creation, underscoring the necessity of representation and inclusivity to ensure equitable and responsible AI deployment. Practical applications are brought to life through case studies, such as streamlining e-commerce operations by optimizing order-processing workflows with persona-driven responses. Furthermore, it explores how tailoring outputs to align with user demographics and preferences, exemplified through the audience persona pattern, can enhance communication and engagement. This approach represents a paradigm shift in AI-user interactions, offering a dynamic, adaptable framework for achieving highly personalized and responsive AI behavior.

Keywords: Audience persona pattern, Ethical AI design, Language models, Natural Language Processing (NLP), Persona patterns, Tailored responses.

INTRODUCTION

That was a digression into technical details, because, further down the rabbit hole of language models, you will find the fascinating phenomenon of persona patterns, which is a foundational improvement for these entities. Deep Dive into Persona Patterns — In this chapter, we dive deep into persona patterns and how they can influence language models. We hope you enjoy the nuances of persona patterns as much as we do and discover their unexplored extension to the domain of natural language processing.

Sumit Tripathi

Persona patterns, however, mark a paradigm shift in the way GPTs operate and provide an unlikely opportunity to embed rich perspectives and zappy knowledge in the outputs they generate. In contrast with traditional methods that utilize fixed datasets and algorithms, persona patterns add another dimension to the mix by replicating the perspectives and knowledge of people in different scenarios. Persona patterns are used to enable language models to respond as if they are experienced professionals, eager learners, or sceptical critics, which helps them tailor their responses to suit different situations.

PERSONA PATTERNS: WHAT ARE THEY AND WHY DO YOU NEED THEM?

To understand the intricacies of persona patterns, you need to explore the underlying tenets and workings of persona patterns. In its most basic form, a persona pattern is a template for instilling language models with unique traits, such as subject matter knowledge, personality, and manner of speaking [1]. Through carefully curated personas based on particular roles or perspectives, language models gain the ability to produce responses that are relatable to a target audience, allowing for interactions that are more engaging and relevant. This flexibility in persona patterns examples is the exact complement of perpetual stitching beyond the limit. They allow language models to have multiple personas, whether experts in niche domains or curious newcomers to novel topics. The use of machine learning algorithms and natural language processing techniques allows a high degree of flexibility in the types of questions an AI chatbot can answer. The pattern of Personas allows for knowledge to be absorbed from multiple sources so that the language model can use it depending on the context.

Persona patterns are thus a flexible means of shaping language model outputs, whether conveying precisely detailed analyses of complex scientific principles or commenting lightly on more quotidian matters. This flexibility allows language models to dynamically manipulate their persona traits, making them more effective at producing responses that are contextually relevant and finely attuned to particular audiences. Persona patterns are essential in enhancing how language models adapt and respond to a range of common contexts [2].

How to Use Persona Patterns in Practice

Persona patterns can lead to better interactions using language models in many domains and applications. And the magic happens thanks to persona patterns, which enable developers and researchers to define personalized experiences based on the individual requirements of users. In a domain like customer service, persona patterns could help create personas of different types of customers — tech-enthusiasts and novices asking for help. Fig. (1) shows the processing of persona patterns in prompt engineering. In addition, persona patterns can be utilized to overcome particular issues in natural language processing, like alleviating bias and understanding context.

Fig. (1). Working of Persona Patterns.

Diversity in Data: Diversity in data refers to the importance of ensuring a wide range of perspectives and viewpoints are included in the data used to train language models. Further, persona patterns allow language models to better understand context, generating more relevant and accurate responses depending on the user engagement setting [3].

Creating Persona Patterns

The persona patterns are carefully set according to the different needs of the target audience, the use case in mind, and the desired expertise or specialization level. There should be a step-by-step process to identifying some key aspects of personality like knowledge, individual and communication style, creating effective trees for the persona patterns [4]. When this characteristic has been described, the developers should integrate it into the process of training the language model, ensuring that this model learns to behave like this persona and respond accordingly [5].

Along with persona characteristics, the developers should also consider the morality of the persona design, as a person would represent a particular audience or voice. Persona patterns should be created responsibly, respecting affinities with relevant factors like representation, pluralism, or intersectionality. This has a positive effect on the quality and integrity of interactions with language models, as long as developers are careful to follow ethical guidelines and best practices in creating persona patterns.

GETTING THE MOST FROM PERSONA PATTERNS

The potential for persona patterning to impact future natural language-based applications becomes ever more clear as we are presented with successive growth of language models. This dataset can be used in a further context of developing large deep-learning models, which can help in working with persona patterns efficiently and effectively. Combining Persona Patterns with other patterns from methods like sentiment analysis and topic modelling may be useful to enrich the results that are generated by language models. Persona patterns are not static, and their future will depend on their evolution and adaptation to changing user needs and preferences. Persona patterns will be key in how language models will also become more advanced and able to create unique, tailored interactions with users, creating more engaging experiences. Using persona pattern knowledge enables language models to move beyond traditional limitations and allows users to shape their interactions with technology from new perspectives

Persona patterns are a paradigm shift in how language models converse with users, providing a dynamic and flexible framework for shaping NLU in the coming years. Persona patterns allow language models to tailor their responses to various contexts and audiences, adding value and relevance to these digital constructs in different fields by characterizing viewpoints and domains of experience. The journey with persona patterns has only just begun, and we are excited to see how it will unfold in the future, revolutionizing the way we create and experience technology in the modern world.

CASE STUDY: USING PROMPT ENGINEERING TO AUTOMATE ORDER PROCESSING

Problem Statement

ABC Electronics, an online consumer electronics retailer, faces delays and inefficiency in its call ordering system. On a daily basis, the company fails to keep up with a large number of orders, resulting in missing orders, increased shipping times, and ultimately, unhappy customers. The Challenge: ABC Electronics wants to cut down on the time spent on processing orders and do the work more efficiently.

Solution: Optimizing Order Processing with Prompt Engineering

Identifying the Problem

The company analyses and identifies pain points in its order processing system, such as manual order entry, real-time lack of inventory visibility, and communication gaps between departments. These inefficiencies lead to delays in order fulfilment and sub-optimal customer experience.

Defining Persona Patterns

By applying the principles of prompt engineering, ABC Electronics creates persona patterns to target various stages of their order processing workflow. These patterns may include things like a proactive inventory manager, a detail-oriented order processor, or a responsive customer service representative. The point of every persona is to ensure that they address certain pain points and help to work smartly.

Automation Tools Implementation

ABC Electronics combines automation tools and software solutions to minimize repetitive administrative tasks and automate tasks within the order processing workflows. How order entry is done automatically naturally accesses the order site and imports the order-related information into the database of the enterprise, instead of manual data input errors; the order entry time is greatly shortened, and orders are filled quickly.

Improving Inventory Management

ABC Electronics uses persona patterns to implement proactive inventory management strategies that ensure optimal stock levels, minimizing the risk of stockouts. The proactive inventory manager persona also uses predictive analytics and demand forecasting techniques to forecast inventory needs and reorder products before they run out to ensure seamless order fulfilment.

Enhancing Communication Lines

To facilitate effective coordination, ABC Electronics establishes clear communication channels between the departments involved in the order processing workflow, such as sales, inventory management, and shipping. When it comes to effective communication, it is the usage of the persona patterns that the company uses, making sure company data is readily available before order processing delays and other human errors take place.

Monitoring and Optimization

Through the use of data analytics tools, ABC Electronics regularly tracks KPIs like order processing times, inventory turnover rates, and customer satisfaction scores. Using the insights from these metrics, it iteratively improves its persona patterns, automation processes, and communications to achieve further efficiency in order processing.

RESULTS

Using prompt engineering principles to enhance its order processing operations, ABC Electronics experiences dramatic improvements in efficiency and customer satisfaction:

Faster Processing Times

Automation techniques and improved workflows allow quicker processing times, enhancing ABC Electronics' capacity to respond to customer needs and to fulfill orders in a timely manner.

Enhanced Inventory Management

With proactive inventory management strategies, businesses can avoid stockouts and overstocking as products are always available in quantities when an order is placed, leading to fewer backorders and improved inventory turnover.

Improved Customer Satisfaction

Efficient order fulfilment and proactive communication result in improved customer satisfaction levels, fostering repeat business and positive word-of-mouth recommendations.

As a result, prompt engineering becomes a powerful ally for ABC Electronics in their quest for efficient order processing, ensuring a seamless shopping experience for their customers. Through innovative technology, proactive communication, and constant improvements, the company positions itself as a leader in efficient order fulfillment in the electronics retail sector.

Enable Sentences for Streamlining Order Processing

Using persona patterns in order processing is a strategic and powerful tool in terms of systems, as systems tend to follow a certain trend; the best configurations will behave similarly under similar conditions. This chapter explores the nuances of persona patterns; how intentionally designing and utilizing well-defined personas can dramatically improve the efficiency of the order processing workflow. This level of detailing enables businesses to formulate strategies specific to each persona, thus improving efficiency and ensuring high standards of customer experience. So now we can start walking through the persona patterns at work for order processing to show how this approach can reshape the complex processes of order fulfillment.

What is an Inventory Manager for Proactive Inventory?

This persona keeps an eye on stock levels, forecasts demand, and restocks as necessary. This position entails more strategic duties like demand forecasting and sales analysis in addition to basic stock management duties. In order to determine which products are popular and when they would likely gain a market, the persona uses sales analysis to look at past data and find sales patterns. This study serves as the foundation for comprehending future demand, in which the appropriate products are offered at the appropriate moment.

To maintain ideal inventory levels, the persona puts orders with vendors based on these projections. This proactive strategy helps avoid overstocking, which can tie up cash and raise storage expenses, and stockouts, which can result in lost sales opportunities. More effective supply chain management and cost control are made possible by the persona's capacity to precisely predict demand and place orders on time. In order to maintain the company's responsiveness to shifting consumer demands, they might also coordinate with the marketing and sales divisions to balance stock levels brought on by sales, promotions, or market swings.

The Detail-oriented Order Processor

This persona is in charge of correctly processing incoming orders, confirming order information, and getting orders ready for delivery. From receiving the initial request to making sure the package is sent appropriately, their function guarantees that every order is handled quickly. To prevent errors that can cause delays or unhappy customers, the persona verifies the correctness of order facts, including product specs, quantities, and customer information.

The persona in question frequently works with data, including inventory records and order information, in addition to processing orders. They make sure that the stock levels are appropriately updated and update the inventory records to reflect the items sold. This procedure is essential for keeping an accurate inventory and avoiding inconsistencies that can influence orders in the future. The persona also handles the warehousing personnel's selection, packing, and shipping of the appropriate merchandise. To ensure that order fulfillment runs smoothly, the personification might frequently expedite urgent orders or discuss certain difficulties with warehouse staff. The persona could generate fictitious responses that are dependent on real-time information, including order details, inventory updates, or warehouse coordination. These answers provide insight into how the persona oversees daily operations, making sure that every facet of the order process is efficiently managed and that client happiness is always given first priority.

Customer Service Representative Responsive

This persona is intended to respond to any questions consumers may have about their orders, including debugging order problems and giving them regular order progress updates. In essence, they always want to make sure that clients have a great experience, particularly if they have questions regarding their order or are attempting to fix any problems that may arise. They must respond in a timely, accurate, and helpful manner so that they feel heard and taken into consideration at every stage of the procedure. Among the persona's duties are answering commonly asked questions (FAQs), which may involve requesting additional details from clients in order to inquire about the progress of an order. They are in charge of informing clients about the progress of their orders, including any delays, shipment details, and delivery dates. When it comes to resolving order concerns or fixing problems like incorrect item shipment, missing parcels, or damaged goods, this other persona is crucial. They assist in promptly resolving problems to ensure client satisfaction and avoid escalation.

The person's frequently asked questions (FAQs) are likely to address inquiries, clarify product information, help with returns or exchanges, and give clients instructions on how to track their orders. They should respond to consumer complaints or issues as soon as possible in the hopes of coming up with a workable and agreeable solution. Therefore, the persona makes sure that a customer's complaint is handled properly and immediately, which promotes loyalty and trust.

Shipping Coordinator – Efficient

In order to guarantee that purchases are shipped to clients in a timely and accurate manner, this role supervises the shipping and delivery procedure. To guarantee that deliveries arrive on schedule and in pristine shape, this entails liaising with logistics suppliers, creating shipping labels, and monitoring packages along their delivery journey. To find the most economical and effective delivery options, the persona collaborates closely with logistics companies. This entails picking reliable carriers, haggling over shipping costs, and making sure the tools required for a seamless delivery are on hand. Another crucial aspect of this job is making precise shipping labels, which guarantee that items are monitored and addressed appropriately from the time they leave the warehouse until they reach their destination.

To be able to keep track of parcels and spot any delays or issues that can occur during delivery, the persona also tracks packages. The character proactively coordinates with logistics providers or clients to resolve any issues that may emerge, such as delayed deliveries. By closely monitoring the shipping and delivery procedure, the persona makes sure that clients receive their orders as promised, which enhances customer happiness and creates a great customer experience.

Data-driven Analyst

This persona applies data analytics tools and techniques to analyse order processing metrics, identify bottlenecks, and recommend process enhancements.

Persona responses include tracking KPIs, creating reports, and making data-driven recommendations to optimize order processing workflows.

Weighted by the processes presented on the journey they go through, the persona patterns focus on various parts of the entire order processing workflow — from inventory management to order processing, customer service, and shipping coordination. These powerful persona patterns will help ABC Electronics leverage its order processing, optimize its operations, and provide a better customer experience.

THE AUDIENCE PERSONA PATTERN: CUSTOMIZING OUTPUTS

The audience persona pattern is an especially powerful tool for tailoring outputs produced by large language models. This chapter reveals the subtleties of this pattern, showing how it gives users a way to tailor content for specific groups or individual users. The addition of the audience persona pattern allows users to shape the tone, style, and emphasis of the content produced to better reflect the distinctive traits and interests of their desired audience. Such a tailored approach guarantees that the context is more impactful with information presented in a contextually relevant fashion based on recipient requirements. In this chapter, the audience persona pattern shows how it could substantially improve how relevant and impactful outputs from large language models can be and lay the groundwork for the future of personalized and audience-specific communication.

Audience Persona Pattern

The audience persona pattern enables users to instruct large language models to produce outputs suited to a specific audience or individual. While existing approaches impose rules/constraints for content generation, this pattern focuses on profiling the target audience of the information. Users utilize this pattern by sharing the demographics, interests, and preferences of their audience, enabling them to adjust the results of the model to effectively engage their target demographic. This more nuanced, situational, and flexible approach recognizes that information consumers are not all the same, and that tailoring content to their context improves communication and leads to understanding. The first track helps users establish a lead for the process through using this audience persona pattern where it provides the initial output but users need to work with the model and fine-tune the outputs to match different aspects of the audience like its demographics and psychographics that affect the way of communication from both the ends; all in an attempt to make every communication meaningful and powerful.

Implementation

This pattern of addressing the audience (audience persona) can be easily activated by the users; here they need to specify the general audience, or a specific audience to whom we need to generate the output. Users can specify traits on the intended audience, including age, expertise level, interests, or profession, or even allude to historical figures. This lens facilitates communication with the model on how to package content to resonate with that user (or demographic). This simplifies the task as the output will then be generated according to the identifying persona on all scales, resulting in context-relevant and in-depth content that will lead it to be more relatable to the right audience. By requiring only a few simple steps (using an audience persona pattern), the user can seamlessly enable the audience persona pattern directly for this prompt, thus also increasing the practicality of using this to match outputs with a range of very specific audience segments.

Example Scenarios

Persona 1: No CS Background Layperson

Query: "Explain large language models and how they work to me. Pretend that I know nothing about computer science."

Output: No jargon, and it uses familiar analogies for a non-technical audience to understand what large language models are. It emphasizes how language models can be utilized in real-world settings like voice assistance and conversational agents.

Persona 2: Historical Figure — Christopher Columbus

This works best for: "Explain large language models and how they work to me. Imagine that I am Christopher Columbus."

Output: Based on its training data and an understanding of their time period and limited knowledge of current technology, the model weaves a story about magical scribes that can predict the future in a way resembling exploratory endeavours. It paints large language models as virtual scribes who are "able to comprehend and replicate human language, personalized to elicit sympathy for the persona of Christopher Columbus."

Persona 3: 2nd Grader with Short Attention Span

Question: "Explain large language models and how they work to me. Assume that I am a second grader who is easily bored."

Output: The model does remain a bit playful, recounting a narrative of sorts that compares large language models to a robot friend that is good at word games. By incorporating interactive storytelling and highlighting the model's capacity to complete sentences, respond to inquiries, and narrate tales, it captures the attention and interests of a youthful audience.

The audience persona pattern provides a general mechanism to adapt outputs from large language models to the needs of different audiences and preferences. "Using insight into the audience helps produce engaging, understandable, and pertinent text. The audience persona pattern enables users to realize the aspect of a large language model in communicating and disseminating information, whether in a complex concept explanation or storytelling.

ILLUSTRATION OF AUDIENCE PERSONA PATTERN IN PERSONALIZED MARKETING CAMPAIGN

Scenario

A multinational e-commerce company is optimizing marketing strategies through Audience Persona Pattern. The company's wide variety of products means they want to create more targeted campaigns that reach their diverse customers in a personal way.

Implementation

The marketing team opts to leverage the Audience Persona Pattern to create in-depth personas for the audience. They then guide the large language model to produce tailored questions that will enable segmentation of customer groups based on their unique characteristics, preferences, and behaviours. These involve demographics, purchase history, interests, preferred method of communication, and other relevant leads.

Example Interaction

Let us kick this off with the marketing team: "Who are our potential customers for the upcoming fitness equipment launch?"

Audience Persona Pattern: It generates follow-up questions like "What age group do you want to target? "Are they more prone to shop online or in brick-an--mortar?" "They are interested in what category of fitness?"

Outcome

The responses come from marketing team members who, to answer them, rely on what they know about their target audience, plus what they glean by doing market research. The Audience Persona Pattern deepens the understanding of customer segments, allowing the team to develop detailed personas for diverse demographics. For example, they segment the population into groups based on exercise frequency and identify a young, digital-native segment of customers who shop online and enjoy new-age fitness devices.

Marketing Campaign

With this level of detail in their audience personas, the marketing team can tailor their campaigns accordingly. They design ads for this segment about the tech aspects and the convenience of the fitness equipment. At the same time, they create in-store promotions for another segment that favours a hands-on shopping experience.

RESULTS

These personalized marketing campaigns, informed by the Audience Persona Pattern, drive higher engagement and conversions. They have also been seeing higher clickthrough rates for online ads and increased foot traffic in their physical stores, illustrating the effectiveness of targeted communication based on audience preferences.

Key Takeaways

The Audience Persona Pattern supports building rich and accurate audience personas.

Examine detailed customer segments by asking specific questions.

By creating tailored marketing campaigns based on these well-defined personas, they can be far more effective with increased engagement and conversion rates.

The Audience Persona Pattern: How does it work in a Marketing Context? The audience persona pattern is basically used to enhance the effectiveness of campaigns by tailoring them to the specific preferences and characteristics of diverse customer segments.

CONCLUSION

This chapter illustrates how persona patterns can improve the flexibility and applicability of language models in a wide range of contexts. Allowing language models to take on a variety of personas enables AI systems to more effectively adapt their responses to particular user circumstances, enhancing interaction functionality and engagement. Beyond enriching the user experience, persona patterns also address key challenges in natural language processing, such as mitigating bias, improving context comprehension, and enabling greater personalization. However, the chapter stresses that designing and applying persona patterns requires a conscientious and ethical approach. Careful attention must be given to ensure these personas are inclusive, respectful, and reflective of diverse perspectives. Poorly designed patterns risk perpetuating harmful biases, whereas responsible implementation can help foster fairness and equity in AI interactions. Looking ahead, the development of persona patterns is poised to drive further innovation, paving the way for more nuanced and highly personalized AI-driven experiences. As illustrated by case studies—such as optimizing order management systems and enhancing targeted marketing strategies—persona patterns hold transformative potential across industries by delivering more precise, efficient, and user-centric AI solutions.

REFERENCES

[1] Y. Chang, Y. Lim, and E. Stolterman, "Personas: From theory to practices", In: Proceedings of the 5th Nordic conference on Human-computer interaction: building bridges ACM: Lund Sweden: *Association for Computing Machinery*, 2008, pp. 439–442. [http://dx.doi.org/10.1145/1463160.1463214]

[2] B.J. Jansen, J.O. Salminen, and S.G. Jung, "Data-driven personas for enhanced user understanding: Combining empathy with rationality for better insights to analytics", *Data Inf. Manag.*, vol. 4, no. 1, pp. 1-17, 2020.

[http://dx.doi.org/10.2478/dim-2020-0005]

[3] J. White, "A prompt pattern catalog to enhance prompt engineering with ChatGPT", Feb. 21, 2023. [http://dx.doi.org/10.48550/arXiv.2302.11382]

[4] M. Zheng, J. Pei, L. Logeswaran, M. Lee, and D. Jurgens, "When 'a helpful assistant' is not really helpful: personas in system prompts do not improve performances of large language models", Oct. 09, 2024. [http://dx.doi.org/10.48550/arXiv.2311.10054]

[5] N. Nananukul, K. Sisaengsuwanchai, and M. Kejriwal, "Cost-efficient prompt engineering for unsupervised entity resolution in the product matching domain", *Discover Artificial Intelligence,* vol. 4, no. 1, p. 56, 2024. [http://dx.doi.org/10.1007/s44163-024-00159-8]

CHAPTER 6

Dynamic Conversation Strategies: Cognitive Verifier, Question Crafting, and Flipped Interaction

Abstract: The Cognitive Verifier Pattern, Question Crafting, and Flipped Interaction represent three sophisticated conversational strategies designed to enhance user engagement with Large Language Models (LLMs), as analyzed in this chapter. Each approach serves as a distinct pathway to elevate conversations in terms of quality, depth, and accuracy. The Cognitive Verifier Pattern focuses on deconstructing complex queries into smaller, more manageable components, enabling users to generate comprehensive and precise responses. The Question Crafting strategy emphasizes iterative refinement, empowering users to progressively enhance the effectiveness of their inquiries. Meanwhile, the Flipped Interaction model redefines traditional user-system dynamics by actively involving users in the conversation—encouraging them to co-create responses and prompting the system to pose clarifying questions. The chapter provides practical illustrations of how these strategies can be implemented in real-world scenarios, such as improving educational experiences and optimizing individual decision-making processes. In its conclusion, the chapter underscores the critical role these approaches play in fostering more efficient, meaningful, and interactive communication between humans and AI systems.

Keywords: Conversational AI, Cognitive verifier pattern, Dynamic dialogue strategies, Flipped interaction, Interactive learning, Question crafting.

INTRODUCTION

The art and science of conversational design is hiding between these lines; it is the close-up process with multiple strategies that makes the conversation animated, like in a few examples above. This chapter, called 'Strategies for Dynamic Conversations: Cognitive Verification, Question Crafting, and Flipped Interaction,' broadens our experience of the nuances in conversational landscapes through the framing of three important patterns. From the first section on Cognitive Verifier Pattern, we cover rigorous approaches to cross-checking, verification, and establishing trust within conversational interactions. In this chapter, the author transitions to the fine art of Question Crafting, emphasizing

Sumit Tripathi

that effective questioning articulation becomes a fulcrum for honing conversations to specificity and pertinence [1]. This journey leads to the Flipped Interaction pattern, revealing a way to reverse the conventional roles between users and systems, progressively framing more advanced patterns of interactive dialogues with users. Readers will learn practical takeaways, examples, and considerations for successfully executing these strategies along the way [2]. Incorporating aspects of information validation, deepening questioning finesse, or leaning into inverted exchanges — talk design is a nuanced microcosm, and this chapter is ultimately a reference point for navigating these dimensions of conversational interaction and addressing the complexities of engagement-driven reality [3].

The Process of Question Refinement

The question refinement pattern is a strategic process in which each iteration of a question builds upon and improves the previous one, making it clearer, more specific, and more relevant to the answer. In this technique, poorly worded or imprecise questions are refined with the help of a high-level language model. Utilizing the features of a large language model, users can iteratively phrase and rephrase their inquiries until the most accurate and relevant information extraction is achieved. This approach allows for questions that may not have been perfectly articulated to begin with — something we've seen time and again around this project — because we don't know the exact questions, the really unknown unknowns, until we start exploring. Internet search, for instance, allows users to iteratively refine their questions, taking advantage of the model's ability to understand and generate language to craft increasingly precise questions [4]. This, along with the question refinement pattern, enables users to formulate the most relevant request to the language model and receive the most impactful results. This idea of iterative improvement of queries encourages users to participate in the optimization of queries, a partnership between the human operator and the language model to improve the effectiveness of communication and knowledge manipulation. In summary, the question-refinement pattern is an iterative process, and refining our questions is a key aspect of using the inner dialog — with the language model as well as with ourselves — to achieve the best possible user experience.

Implementation

A common way to implement the first-question-refinement pattern is for the user to instruct the large language model to improve the quality of subsequent queries [5]. When a user asks a question and receives an answer, the model processes the request iteratively, generating better versions of the original question. It may be providing context, going deeper on parameters, or requesting more specific identifying features to clarify and narrow the query. The user is shown an updated version of that query and can then choose whether to use the suggested upgrade or to keep their original request.

Example 1

Instead of asking a general question like "What is the weather like today?", a more refined approach could be to ask, "What is the detailed weather forecast for me, including temperature, precipitation, and wind conditions?" This refined query helps gather more specific and accurate information, guiding the model to provide a deeper, more meaningful answer.

Example 2

Initial query: "Tell me about artificial intelligence."

Rephrased question: "Can you give us a summary of recent developments in artificial intelligence, especially in healthcare, and how they may affect patient outcomes?"

Once again, the original question is quite vague, but the refined question is specific to recent AI advancements and limited to a specific field (healthcare), making it more targeted and likely to yield relevant information.

Example 3

Original question: "How do I improve my writing skills?"

Refined question: "At my current proficiency level, what things would you recommend to me in order to improve both my creative and technical writing skills: strategies, resources, *etc.*?"

The second question is phrased more intentionally; it asks not just at what level the user is currently at in terms of creative versus technical writing, but it also prompts the user to disclose which, even if they might consider more of a strength or focus at the moment, they might have also coined a recent thought. This provides you with a more tailored and actionable answer. The role of the question-refinement pattern, illustrated by these examples, is to convert an unanswered question or a vague inquiry into a more coherent and contextualized question, resulting in an answer that is more informative and illuminating.

Extension Work Case Study with Emphasis on Filter Question Theme: Improving College Decision Process

Scenario

Emily is a high school senior facing the difficult decision of which university to attend for her undergraduate degree. Overwhelmed, she uses the question-refinement pattern to obtain more personalized information from the large language model.

Initial Question

"What is the best college for me?"

Language Model Generated Refined Question

"Outside of academics, what are some aspects I should be looking for when deciding on a college, such as campus culture, financial aid, the number of extracurriculars, and the programs? How do I square these with my career objectives and personal likes?"

Outcome

The make-sense clause prompts Emily to consider her priorities and preferences more thoroughly. The model's suggestions make her think about what she wants in a college outside of "best," opening up a wider exploration of choices.

Further Interaction

However, after the question was transformed, American-born Emily took it a level deeper. She says, "Are you able to give me some specific details about each university's academic programs relating to environmental science and sustainability on my list?"

Answer Refined (As per A Model)

"Sure! So, on to the environmental science and sustainability programs at the schools you have on your radar. We will examine the faculty expertise, courses offered, research opportunities, and any other unique aspects of their programs for each university."

Outcome

Emily receives detailed insights curated specifically for her educational pursuits. This iterative refinement cycle has not only made her questions much clearer but also led to more focused and pertinent responses.

Final Decision

Through some back and forth of well-articulated inquiries and fleshed-out answers, Emily is armed with a ton of information. As the university she chooses meets her academic and personal criteria, this illustrates how the question-refinement pattern led to more informed decision-making.

Key Takeaways

The question refinement pattern helps users break down complex decision points into concrete questions that can be actioned. This leads users to think from many angles and supports a personalized, integrated approach to problem-solving.

The output depends on the inputs, so each subsequent use provides a new layer of feedback and the questions keep developing, yielding increasingly relevant and useful insights.

THE COGNITIVE VERIFIER PATTERN

The cognitive verifier pattern defers to the strategic approach of breaking complex problems into subcomponents to enable the large language model to do more, supplementing the question refinement pattern [6]. This approach acknowledges that many multidimensional problems or inquiries can be adequately addressed by breaking them down into simpler, more narrowly focused pieces. This means breaking down a user query into multiple individual questions or sub-problems. It enables users to canvas individual components of the broader problem space in greater detail. This way, the model is able to give more precise and thorough answers for each sub-component, resulting in a better understanding of the whole problem. In contrast, the cognitive verifier pattern is useful for complex queries that include multiple dimensions or need deep analysis. This promotes users to break down complex issues and look at each piece or component in a more structured and focused way. This helps to provide accurate information and also enables users to understand the complexities of the subject. The cognitive verifier pattern complements the question refinement pattern, and together they create an immersive user experience that promotes step-by-step analysis of complex problems [7]. Uplift Inquiries — By breaking questions down into smaller pieces, users can approach complex subjects with more precision, resulting in enhanced accuracy and depth in responses from the large language model.

Key Concepts in Cognitive Verifier Pattern

Decomposition: Dividing a complex question into smaller components.

Sub-questions: Sub-questions are focused questions that answer certain facets of the overall issue.

Synthesis: Putting together replies to sub-questions to provide a comprehensive solution.

Implementation

The third cognitive verifier pattern: Users task the large language model with expanding their inquiry by generating further questions. These additional questions help to break the problem down into individual, more closely related components. The model is goal-directed attention, which emphasizes relevant factors and contextual details, or fundamental assumptions, and strives to provide the original query with a more complete and sophisticated understanding. Once the user answers these sub-questions, the model compiles all the information to provide a holistic and polished answer to the original question.

Example 1

A user might ask, “What’s the best way to improve my productivity?” The model begins generating questions like, “What kind of tasks do you need to get done?” which follows the cognitive verifier pattern. “Are there certain distractions in your work environment?” and “When do you feel most focused during the day?” So by deconstructing the big productivity picture into these wee bits, the model is able to provide advice that is then unique to the context of the user, providing context to the model, and therefore, much more actionable advice!

Example 2

User Query: “What can I do to minimize my carbon footprint?”

Examples of cognitive verifier questions: “What forms of transportation do you use the most?” "Can you tell me how much energy you use in your home?" "Are you a vegetarian or vegan?" Exploring these sub-questions allows the model to provide tailored recommendations, whether suggesting more sustainable modes of transport, energy-saving methods, or changes to an individual's diet.

Example 3

User query: “Give me an overview of the history of artificial intelligence.”

Cognitive verifier sub-questions: “Would you be focused more on the germinal or the latest developments?” “Do you have a particular application, like AI in health care or robotics?" "So who are you exploring — what figures or historical events?" Answering these sub-questions enables the model to make the overview of the history more relevant to the user, adding a more personalized feel to the exploration of the topic.

These examples highlight how the cognitive verifier pattern can enrich user experience by providing interactive and tailored pathways to query resolution. When faced with complicated questions, the model breaks them down into smaller pieces, resulting in more accurate and relevant answers to each individual part – an example of the cognitive verifier pattern to tackle complex queries.

By using the question refinement pattern and the cognitive verifier pattern, we can significantly improve the quality, depth, and accuracy of the response in interactions with large language models. Users can derive meaningful insights and make better decisions by optimizing questions for clarity and distilling complex challenges into digestible units of analysis. This will be incredibly helpful each time we want to use a large language model to the best of its abilities.

Cognitive Verifier Pattern Case Study: Enhance Your Learning Techniques for Examination

Scenario

Sophia is studying for her finals at college, and she wants to make the most of her study time. To improve her approach, she chooses to use the cognitive verifier pattern.

Initial Inquiry

"How can I study more effectively for my upcoming tests?"

Cognitive Verifier Pattern Usage

Sophia has the large language model that will generate more questions that decompose the main question. The model has responded with several sub-questions: "What subjects are you studying?" "What's your preferred way to learn?" "How many hours can you afford to study every day?" Sophia replies, specifying her subjects and answers, indicating her preferred style of learning and hours available to study.

Refined Response

The model absorbs this information and then offers personalized recommendations, like developing visual tools that are easier to grasp, using the

Pomodoro method to lose hit spaces appropriately, and linking to study materials specifically suited for that topic. The improved answer provides a more personalized and actionable plan tailored to Sophia's specific situation.

Outcome

Sophia uses the filtered study strategies recommended by the model. Focusing on particular study elements and her tastes, her findings showed that she now studies in a more focused style and much more efficiently. The cognitive verifier pattern has not only provided pertinent guidance but also enabled Sophia to customize her exam preparation to her own requirements.

Key Takeaways

The cognitive verifier pattern invites users to decompose their primary question into concrete parts.

It should then ask follow-up questions for further details to customize model suggestions.

It also means users get refined and actionable advice, making problem-solving or decision-making much more effective.

This case study exemplifies the cognitive verifier pattern in the domain of study strategy optimization. The model can digest general questions and respond to specific queries based on narrowed-down dimensions, which provides a more tailored recommendation to the user on how to tackle complex questions.

FLIPPED INTERACTION PATTERN

With its shift away from the traditional meaning of user-computer interaction, the Flipped Interaction Pattern redefines how users engage with large language models. In general, users tend to come to systems looking for information or help, and the model is reactive, sitting back and waiting for a prompt from the user before providing a response [8]. In contrast, the Flipped Interaction Pattern represents a change in mindset where users are encouraged to become more active and involved in the interaction. In contrast to the historical one-way information flow, the Flipped Interaction Pattern creates a two-way dynamic, where users are not only searching for solutions but are also actively assisting in the generation and perfection of content. This reciprocal exchange turns the user from simply a recipient of information into an active co-creator of knowledge. Users are invited to direct the conversation, steering the interaction in the direction they'd like by asking clarifying questions, adding more context, or refining responses [9].

Flipped interaction pattern on types of articles provided is a pattern in which users take charge of the knowledge exchange process. This means users are not just relying on the model's capabilities; the responsibility for the quality and relevance of what they receive lies in the users' hands. This two-way communication not only improves the user experience but also signifies a more democratic and inclusive approach to information sharing [10].

The Flipped Interaction Pattern is a game-changing paradigm shift in the relationship between user and computer interaction. This pattern not only replaces the conventional periphery of participation but also nurtures a diverse, collaborative method of knowledge sharing by encouraging users to rise as active participants and contributors. These patterns turn the question-answer dynamic on its head by requiring the large language model to do the questioning. Instead of posing questions to the user, though, the model takes on the role of an interrogator, drawing responses and information from the user. And it is this flipping of the interaction dynamic that allows users to navigate uncertainty, pursue direction, and experiment with shared solutions.

Implementation

Users use a large language model prompt to ask them questions about a topic or objective to start the flipped interaction pattern. The goal, in turn, allows for the generation of logical, consistent steps that lead toward the desired direction; in this case, the question-generation process will end with an answer that reflects the defined goal. This pattern serves multiple use cases, from problem-solving to decision-making to information retrieval.

EXAMPLE SCENARIOS

Fitness Regimen Design

Scenario

"Ask me questions about my fitness goals until you have enough to suggest a strength-training regimen for me. Hit me with the strength training program once you have enough info. Ask me the first question."

Execution

The model launches into a rapid-fire of questions regarding the user's goals, likes, and dislikes.

The model asks a series of pertinent questions — including the user's specific fitness objective, existing medical conditions, frequency of workout, and access to fitness equipment.

The AI creates an entire strength-training routine based on the user's answers, filling in exercises to meet specific requirements and goals.

After the questioning is complete, the model delivers a custom strength training schedule to the user based on their needs.

Diagnostic Inquiry

Scenario

Query data: "Please ask me questions to diagnose a technical issue with my computer until you have enough information to recommend a solution. Ask me the first question."

Execution

Based on the problem presented, the model starts posing a series of diagnostic questions to determine the hardware and software configuration of the computer, as well as any recent changes made to the computer.

By asking iteratively, the model is ready with relevant information on symptoms, error messages, recent updates, and user behaviour.

Depending on the user's answers, the model generates an initial diagnosis and recommends potential solutions or troubleshooting steps.

After conducting the diagnostic inquiry, the model presents the user with actionable recommendations to effectively resolve the technical issue. Flipped interaction pattern: a versatile tool for enabling inquiry, problem solving, and decision making with large-language models. This approach allows users to leverage the computational abilities of the model, its domain knowledge, and its ability to probe complex issues—with opposing viewpoints, leading to bespoke solutions. Flipped Interaction Pattern: Using the flipped interaction pattern, users can leverage the expertise of large language models to achieve their goals, whether it be by designing fitness regimes, diagnosing a technical issue, or enabling interactive learning.

Case Study: Flipped Interaction Pattern: Co-creation in Content Development

Scenario

An online learning platform is applying the Flipped Interaction Pattern to improve the learner experience for users learning about various topics. This platform integrates with a large language model to enable users to become active participants in content development rather than passive recipients of information.

Implementation

Users are invited to do more than pose a question; the prompts ask them to include background information, clarify how much detail they would like, and add related topics. The Flipped Interaction Pattern is used by the platform to engage users in generating and improving responses. This participatory approach is well-suited to a large language model, fostering a collaborative ecosystem.

Example Interaction

User: "Explain quantum mechanics."

Flipped Interaction: The model replies with an overview before prompting, "Are you interested in the historical development, specific principles, or applications of quantum mechanics? Please provide more detail to customize the response to your application."

User: "I'm curious to know the applications, especially in computing."

Route Reversal Interaction: The system generates some bespoke content with respect to the user's specified interest, "Do you have certain questions around quantum computing, or do you want a general overview?

Outcome:

This iterative, cooperatively informed cycle allows users to refine the specificity of their expectations for information. This pattern of flipped interaction not only shows users content relevant to them, but also allows them to help direct the flow of the experience.

Key Takeaways

Users are sometimes passive consumers rather than active contributors.

Users help generate content by providing context and user preferences, and by improving their queries.

This pattern, collaborating with users, has created a good user experience by tailoring information to their needs and preferences.

In this case study, we see a successful implementation of the Flipped Interaction Pattern and its contribution to creating more active and participatory learning environments, allowing users to influence the information they engage with on the platform.

CONCLUSION

Three dynamic conversational strategies—Cognitive Verifier, Question Crafting, and Flipped Interaction—are highlighted in this chapter for their transformative potential. By enabling users to maximize their interaction with Large Language Models (LLMs), these strategies promote more accurate, pertinent, and captivating conversations. The Cognitive Verifier strategy enables users to deconstruct complex questions, resulting in more specific and actionable responses. The Question Crafting approach encourages iterative refinement of queries, enhancing their clarity and focus to generate higher-quality answers. Lastly, the Flipped Interaction strategy repositions users as active co-creators rather than passive participants, cultivating a more collaborative and tailored conversational experience. By incorporating these strategies, LLMs can offer responses that are better aligned with individual needs, more insightful, and deeply contextualized. As AI technology advances, these innovative strategies will be integral to enhancing user interactions and expanding the potential of conversational AI systems across diverse fields.

REFERENCES

[1] D. Lee, and E. Palmer, "Prompt engineering in higher education: a systematic review to help inform curricula", *International Journal of Educational Technology in Higher Education,* vol. 22, no. 1, p. 7, 2025.
[http://dx.doi.org/10.1186/s41239-025-00503-7]

[2] A. Diyab, R.M. Frost, B.D. Fedoruk, and A. Diyab, "Engineered Prompts in ChatGPT for Educational Assessment in Software Engineering and Computer Science", *Educ. Sci. (Basel),* vol. 15, no. 2, p. 156, 2025.
[http://dx.doi.org/10.3390/educsci15020156]

[3] L. Wang, X. Chen, X. Deng, H. Wen, M. You, W. Liu, Q. Li, and J. Li, "Prompt engineering in consistency and reliability with the evidence-based guideline for LLMs", *NPJ Digit. Med.,* vol. 7, no. 1, p. 41, 2024.
[http://dx.doi.org/10.1038/s41746-024-01029-4] [PMID: 38378899]

[4] J.L. Babin, H. Raber, and T.J. Mattingly II, "Prompt Pattern Engineering for Test Question Mapping Using ChatGPT: A Cross-Sectional Study", *Am. J. Pharm. Educ.,* vol. 88, no. 10, p. 101266, 2024.
[http://dx.doi.org/10.1016/j.ajpe.2024.101266] [PMID: 39153573]

[5] J. White, "A Prompt Pattern Catalog to Enhance Prompt Engineering with ChatGPT", Feb. 21, 2023.

[http://dx.doi.org/10.48550/arXiv.2302.11382]

[6] G. Rabby, S. Auer, J. D'Souza, and A. Oelen, "Fine-tuning and Prompt Engineering with Cognitive Knowledge Graphs for Scholarly Knowledge Organization", Sep. 10, 2024. [http://dx.doi.org/10.48550/arXiv.2409.06433]

[7] O. Kramer, and J. Baumann, "Unlocking Structured Thinking in Language Models with Cognitive Prompting", Nov. 30, 2024. [http://dx.doi.org/10.48550/arXiv.2410.02953]

[8] D. López-Villanueva, R. Santiago, and R. Palau, "Flipped Learning and Artificial Intelligence", *Electronics (Basel),* vol. 13, no. 17, p. 3424, 2024. [http://dx.doi.org/10.3390/electronics13173424]

[9] L.S. Lo, "The CLEAR path: A framework for enhancing information literacy through prompt engineering", *J. Acad. Librariansh.,* vol. 49, no. 4, p. 102720, 2023. [http://dx.doi.org/10.1016/j.acalib.2023.102720]

[10] D. Siegle, "Using AI Prompt Engineering to Improve Gifted Students' Questioning", *Gifted Child Today,* vol. 48, no. 1, pp. 68-72, 2025. [http://dx.doi.org/10.1177/10762175241289886]

CHAPTER 7

Dynamic Dialogues: React Prompting and Chain of Thoughts Interaction

Abstract: React Prompting and Chain of Thought (CoT) interaction represent two advanced strategies for improving communication between users and large language models (LLMs). These methodologies aim to make interactions more seamless, adaptive, and contextually informed. React Prompting enables LLMs to incorporate external data and resources in real time, equipping them to provide accurate, up-to-date responses. This approach is particularly effective in scenarios requiring timely information, such as news reports, location-based recommendations, or healthcare guidance. Conversely, the Chain of Thought Interaction method replicates human reasoning by encouraging models to break down complex issues into smaller, more digestible components. This process emphasizes logical, step-by-step problem solving. Together, these methods excel in applications where clarity and precision are critical. The chapter includes practical examples and case studies to demonstrate the efficacy of these approaches. For instance, in health technology and customer support environments, React Prompting delivers relevant, real-time insights, while Chain of Thought enhances decision-making through structured reasoning. By integrating real-time external data capabilities with a focus on logical thought processes, React Prompting and Chain of Thought Interaction complement each other, advancing user engagement and crafting more effective, tailored AI solutions.

Keywords: Chain of Thought Interaction, Conversational AI, Dynamic Dialogue, External Data Integration, React Prompting, Structured Reasoning.

INTRODUCTION

In the world of language models and conversational AI, an intriguing dance occurs: a chorus of prompts and responses that sing a song to each other. In order to delve deeper into the complex realm of "React Prompting," the first chapter explores the ongoing story of "Chain of Thoughts Interaction." In this journey, we do so in the spirit of interactive communication, where a user prompts something, and a language model responds, to share a space of interaction. All the conversations start with a prompt, and that is where React Prompting comes in as the catalyst for the dialogues. We also explore Chain of Thoughts Interaction, where each prompt and response spark a series of related thoughts, forming

Sumit Tripathi

an engaging and dynamic conversation. The back-and-forth nature of the conversation allows for sustaining the flow of the discussion, influencing how things unfold, and establishing a more profound interactional space between users and models.

REACT PROMPTING

Prompting is the discipline that occupies the fulcrum of the user-machine interaction choreography. But what happens when the world is turned upside down, and the machine series not only replies, but spins out an orchestrated overreaction? Welcome to "React Prompting", the world where interactivity and language models meet in a blend of responses and prompts, forming a melody [1]. In this chapter, we embark on a journey into the world of React Prompting, revealing the enchantment that ensues when users prompt, and machines respond in a dialogue. Here, we explore the nuances of how language models respond to user-initiated prompts, turning simple interactions into engaging and meaningful discussions. Join us as we explore the dynamics of React Prompting, peeling back the layers of this sophisticated interaction. It's like redecorating a room, with each search a new colour swatch on the wall and every result a shift in understanding, a tentative hand to the keys.

This shows that while large language models are powerful machine learning models capable of ingesting vast amounts of data, they can run into difficulties if they do not have experience with something. React Prompting serves strategically as a bridge whereby language models can incorporate additional tools into their reasoning processes to overcome these limitations. At its core, React Prompting enables a more conversational approach to interacting with large language models, wherein users not only prompt the model with questions but also with outputs or reactions [2]. This allows the model to augment its own knowledge and produce better outputs through interaction with external tools or resources. Integrating external tools may involve pulling from databases, using APIs, or leveraging purpose-built software. For example, if a user wants to know the latest release in a particular domain, React Prompting can help the language model tap into up-to-date information in external databases, keeping the answer up to date rather than relying on the model to come up with an answer based solely on what it has learned. This leads to a robust model with much greater flexibility and utility. The use of external tools allows these models to be better suited for a wider range of user queries, making them aware of current events and able to provide more contextually relevant and accurate information. In this setting, React Prompting turns models of language — and hence, language models — into more malleable and polymathic tools; specifically, tools that can quickly stretch and augment their factual knowledge-work and reasoning-werk with knowledge that exceeds their original training data set necessarily. Integrating with external tools is a key input mechanism for large language models, and this process is known as React Prompting [3]. This integration not only expands the range of knowledge these models can access but also increases their flexibility and overall efficiency in handling a variety of diverse and dynamic user requests. React prompting allows the model to:

i. Determine the next step in reasoning.
ii. Determine when external data or computations are required.
iii. Use a tool or a data source to find or compute the missing piece.
iv. Integrate the result back into the reasoning process and continue until the assignment is completed.

Example 1 — News Feed Updates in Real-Time

User Prompt

"What are the latest developments in renewable energy?"

React Prompting

This is because it knows the data is up to date: React Prompting. Rather than just using what it knows, it can call external tools like news APIs. It pulls in and includes the latest news articles and coverage of renewable energy, so the user can get up-to-date info in real time.

Enhancement

As a result, React Prompting can prevent the language model from offering outdated data and adjust its responses to the latest advancements in the renewable energy sector.

Yelp: Context can also make a difference.

User Prompt

“What are the trending restaurants near me?"

React Prompting

Based on React Prompting, the language model makes use of data that it learns beyond its fixed knowledge base and interacts with location-based services. It constantly pulls in data about nearby restaurants, and user preferences based on previous interactions, and delivers a personalized offer that takes into account context to suggest relevant restaurants.

Enhancement

Using the latest complete set of data to enhance the knowledge of users — a kind of formative assessment of a kind in knowledge application — React Prompting allows the model to make suggestions not only based on its general knowledge, but also real-time data about the user's local circumstances and contextual preferences.

Case Study: Health Dynamo: React Prompted Dynamic Assisting

Background

A healthtech app utilizes LLM to help users with their health-related queries. Open Health leverages React Prompting to keep the model consistent with the most recent developments in the research, medical community, and health databases.

Scenario

User: "Describe some new developments in diabetes management."

React Prompting Process

Detecting: The model detects that the user has asked for the most current changes to the way diabetes is managed.

React Prompting Activation: The model activates React Prompting when it realizes that it needs real-time data from external health databases, medical journals, and research repositories.

External Incorporation: The model dynamically integrates the latest research and treatment approaches in diabetes management into its framework from outside sources.

Role

Response Enrichment: The user receives a detailed answer rooted in the knowledge model laws stored in it, integrated with the latest findings discussed in the article, thus providing perspectives on recent diabetes advancements and tailored diabetes treatment.

Outcome

Up-to-Date and Precise Guidance: React Prompting ensures the user is provided with information relevant to the latest developments in diabetes management, beyond the boundaries of the original model's training data.

Dynamic SM: Due to the integration of dynamically usable integrated external health-related tools, the app adapts and creates new content based on changing healthcare trends.

Improved User Engagement: Through consistent delivery of timely and tailored healthcare information, users become more engaged and develop trust in the application.

At the heart of React Prompting lies a systemic approach, and in this blog post, we showcase its potential by creating a delightful healthcare application. React Prompting promotes a more informed and empowered healthcare experience by adapting to new tools and the latest health information.

THE MAGIC OF CHAIN OF THOUGHT PROMPTING

Human-Computer Interaction Reinvigorated. In contrast to traditional question-and-answer systems, Chain of Thought Prompting introduces an exceptional layer of involvement in which user prompts serve as the initial sparks of an engaging, adaptive chain of thoughts. Visualize an interactive conversation, where every user prompt serves as a key, unlocking a plethora of related responses that explore deeper layers of the discussion. What is magical about this design is how these interactions are more liquid, allowing the conversation to run on its own with context created by both user and language model [4]. Every single thing in this magical world has its own pulse, and so too does the conversation. It is not just a response to a user prompt, it is a path, a stream of thought built on the previous text. It also creates a sense of conversational continuity, with the language model remaining fluid and adjusting based on what has been previously discussed, much like in engaging conversations. Chain of Thought Prompting transforms Magic into a deeper, more holistic experience for humans interacting with their AIs. It embodies the more nuanced and organic exchange of ideas you would get in an actual dialogue, with each element adding to the overall richness akin to the depth and complexity of human conversation [5].

Why Do We Want to Be Able to Chain Together Our Thoughts?

Instead of using a traditional question-and-answer format, this method attempts to capture the dynamic nature of dialogue: whenever the user asks a question, a cascade of interrelated thought processes is triggered, mirroring everything we understand about human communication, where ideas are exchanged and evolve organically. The intuition is that conversations are not one-off activities, but rather ongoing narratives shaped by context and developing understanding. Through Chain of Thought Prompting, LMs like GPT-3 are enabled to respond to active discourse, simulating a more conversational aspect of human dialogue.

How to Use Chain of Thought Prompting Effectively?

Provide step-by-step reasoning: Always describe intermediate steps that lead to the final solution. Divide the problem into smaller components and explain each.

Match the problem format: Ensure that the examples offered are relevant to the work at hand. The reasoning should directly answer the query.

Include detailed examples: Provide examples that comprehensively show the reasoning process, including edge situations if needed.

Encourage transparency: Before offering an answer, ask the model to explain exactly how it arrived at that result. This removes ambiguity and allows for greater trust while delivering results.

Iterate and refine: After reviewing the explanation for errors or gaps, refine your prompt.

Why Chain of Thought Prompting Matters

The Chain of Thought. In language models, prompting is essential for sound reasoning. The idea is that if a language model follows a logical flow of ideas, it will be more likely to arrive at the correct answer, just as a student who outlines the steps of their reasoning is more likely to do so. This increases the probability that the model will produce the right result by guiding it through the reasoning process. This part will determine whether or not the prompting strategy is effective.

Good Example: *How to Learn*

The best illustrations of the effectiveness of Chain of Thought Prompting are positive ones. These are instances of problems that require reasoning to answer.

Negative Example: *The Cost of Invisibility*

It is necessary to understand the drawbacks of Chain of Thought Prompting without actually utilizing it before providing positive instances. Here, for instance, a prompt merely consists of a list of questions and their responses; it doesn't go into detail about the reasoning behind the replies. Sometimes, incomplete or incorrectly concluded answers result from the omission of essential reasoning components from the cognitive process. Thus, negative examples make clear why proper thinking requires Chain of Thought Prompting.

Why Chain of Thought Prompting Works

Chain of Thought Prompts strikes a mix between clear directions and examples. In this chapter, the model is guided by the use of context-rich messages, explicit instructions, and descriptive prefixes. Chain of Thought Prompting improves the technique of prompting LLMs, whether by providing directions or examples [6]. Users can obtain more accurate and perceptive results by prompting the model to explain its reasoning. In order to achieve more sophisticated and precise outcomes, tasks should be broken down, and the model should be guided to solve difficulties step by step. Building better, more intelligent language models is made possible as we continue to improve our capacity to reason through prompts [7].

EXAMPLE ON CHAIN OF THOUGHTS PROMPTING

Set 1: Without Chain of Thought Reasoning

Question 1: Choosing Between Two Job Offers

Question

"You've received two job offers: one with a higher salary and one with a better work-life balance. Which should you choose?"

Answer

"You should choose the job with the better work-life balance, as it will lead to long-term satisfaction."

Question 2: Deciding What to Have for Dinner

Question

"It's a busy evening, and you're not sure whether to cook dinner or order takeout. What should you do?"

Answer

"Order takeout, as it will save time and effort after a busy day."

Question 3: Deciding Whether to Exercise After Work

Question

"Should you exercise after work or relax at home?"

Answer

"You should exercise after work, as it will improve your health and energy levels."

Question 4: Choosing Between Two Vacation Destinations

Question

"You have two vacation destinations in mind: a beach resort or a mountain retreat. Which one should you choose?"

Answer

"Choose the beach resort, as it offers a relaxing atmosphere and plenty of activities."

Question asked to LLM

Question 5: Deciding Whether to Buy a New Phone

Question

"Should you buy a new phone or continue using your current one?"

Response from LLM: "Buy a new phone, as it has better features and will last longer."

Set 2: With Chain of Thought Reasoning

Question 1: Choosing Between Two Job Offers

Question

"You've received two job offers: one with a higher salary and one with a better work-life balance. Which should you choose?"

Answer

"Let's break down the decision.

Step 1: Consider salary – a higher salary can provide financial security, but it may come with increased stress or longer hours.

Step 2: Consider work-life balance – a better balance may improve your mental health and personal life, but could come with a lower salary.

Step 3: What is your current priority? If financial security is important to you, a higher salary might be better. However, if you value personal time and well-being, the work-life balance job might be a better choice.

Step 4: If the salary difference isn't drastic, choosing work-life balance could lead to long-term happiness and prevent burnout.

Based on this analysis, I would suggest choosing the job with a better work-life balance."

Question 2: Deciding What to Have for Dinner

Question

"It's a busy evening, and you're not sure whether to cook dinner or order takeout. What should you do?"

Answer

"Let's think about it.

Step 1: Consider how much time you have – cooking dinner can take time, but it may be healthier and cheaper.

Step 2: Think about your energy level – after a busy day, cooking might feel like too much effort.

Step 3: What are your priorities? If saving time is more important, ordering takeout is the faster option.

Step 4: If you have some leftover ingredients or a simple recipe, cooking might still be a good option.

Given the time constraints, ordering takeout might be the better option today."

Question 3: Deciding Whether to Exercise After Work

Question

"Should you exercise after work or relax at home?"

Answer

"Let's break down the decision.

Step 1: Consider how you're feeling – if you're tired, it might be better to relax and recover.

Step 2: Think about the benefits of exercise – regular exercise improves health, mood, and energy levels.

Step 3: How important is it to you to stay healthy or maintain a routine? If fitness is a priority, exercise is a good choice.

Step 4: Can you relax after exercising? If you can balance relaxation with physical activity, exercising first might be the best option.

Based on this reasoning, exercising after work will help your health in the long run."

Question 4: Choosing Between Two Vacation Destinations

Question

"You have two vacation destinations in mind: a beach resort or a mountain retreat. Which one should you choose?"

Answer

"Let's evaluate the options.

Step 1: Consider what you want from the vacation – do you want to relax by the beach, or are you looking for outdoor adventures in the mountains?

Step 2: Think about the weather – if you prefer warmer climates, the beach resort might be a better choice.

Step 3: How important is relaxation *vs.* exploration? A beach resort is great for unwinding, while a mountain retreat offers activities like hiking and sightseeing.

Step 4: Also, think about how accessible each destination is and your budget.

If you're looking for rest and sun, the beach resort is ideal. But if you want adventure and nature, the mountain retreat may suit you better.

Considering all factors, I'd suggest the beach resort for a more relaxing experience."

Question asked to LLM

Question 5: Deciding Whether to Buy a New Phone

<u>Question</u>

"Should you buy a new phone or continue using your current one?"

<u>Response from LLM</u>

"Let's break down the decision.

Step 1: How old is your current phone, and how well is it functioning? If your phone is outdated or slowing down, it might be time to upgrade.

Step 2: Consider the features of the new phone – does it offer better performance, camera quality, or battery life?

Step 3: What's your budget for a new phone? Can you afford it, or would it be more beneficial to wait for a better deal or a future model?

Step 4: Do you really need a new phone, or can your current one still serve your needs?

If your phone is outdated and a newer model offers features that better align with your needs, it might be worth upgrading. If not, you could save money by sticking with your current phone for a while longer."

By forcing the language model to follow a series of logical reasoning stages, chain-of-thought prompting enhances its rational process [7]. In the following circumstances, the model response breaks down choices into smaller, more manageable steps, presenting more meaningful responses and finely refined considerations. It results in more thoughtful and well-tailored recommendations and clarifies the justifications for each response. Responses that lack the critical thinking that may make them more pertinent and individualized are frequently less intelligent and simpler when they lack the Chain of Thought logic. The model will produce responses that are far more accurate, deliberate, and contextually relevant when structured reasoning is used, which will improve decision-making support [8].

CASE STUDY: AN EXAMPLE OF APPLYING COT PROMPTING IN CUSTOMER SUPPORT

Background

In order to extract comprehensive and contextual responses from customer support queries, which many language model-powered support systems struggle with, a top e-commerce technology selects Chain of Thought Prompting to advance the reasoning accuracy of its method.

Objective

The general idea is to guide students through a language model so the customer support quality will be elevated beyond just the solution to a detailed explanation of the common problems and their solution.

Implementation

The e commerce giant implements Chain of Thought Prompting in its customer support interface. For example, when a user asks about orders, returns, or product questions, the language model is instructed to show its workings step by step in its responses. This is to add transparency and help clients understand why certain recommendations or actions have been taken.

Positive Outcomes: Higher Customer Satisfaction

The language model generates more informative and detailed responses as customers express greater satisfaction with the customer support service through Chain of Thought Prompting. Users care about the transparency in the reasoning behind support recommendations.

Reduced Follow-Up Queries

Following is a decline in follow-up questions, further reinforcing the effectiveness of Chain of Thought Prompting. The prior responses are more detailed, which results in fewer follow-up or repeated questions by the customers.

Improved User Education

By showing the reasoning behind its answers, the language model serves as an educational tool for the user. Provides customers with information on platform policies and processes to improve their understanding of the system.

Negative Insights: Initial Learning Curve

At first, the customer support agents may need to learn to adapt to the new system, which may take extra time to provide a detailed explanation. That said, this complication declines with repeated usage and practice.

Future Considerations: Integration of User Feedback

It will also continue to be fine-tuned by incorporating user feedback to improve the Chain of Thought Prompting approach.

Expanding Multilingual Support

The initiative recognizes the potential to scale further based on the success seen in the first few iterations and seeks to bring Chain of Thought Prompting to multilingual queries to perform better for a wider audience.

Conclusion

The benefits of Chain of Thought Prompting in improving customer service on an e-commerce platform are illustrated in this case study. By emphasizing clear, thorough reasoning in responses, the language model-driven support system helps improve user education, reduce follow-up inquiries, and boost customer satisfaction. The usefulness of such a Chain of Thought Prompting for improving the calibre of client interactions in the e-commerce sector will undoubtedly increase as the platform continues to improve and expand this strategy.

REACT AND CHAIN OF THOUGHT PROMPTING AS COMPLEMENTARY METHODS

It is important to review the chain of thought prompting, a technique that divides a problem into sequential steps with justifications for each step, before getting into the specifics of React Prompting. This concept is expanded upon by React Prompting, which also uses outside resources to improve problem-solving skills. The two techniques complement each other: both chain of thought prompting and react prompting stress how crucial it is to provide a thorough justification for the argument.

Example 1

For example, chain of thought prompting could mean that when asked a mathematical question, the model explains each step leading up to the calculation. React Prompting, building on this, prompts the model that it may use external tools, such as searching the web or calling APIs for the domain-specific information needed to accomplish the task.

Example 2

For instance, consider a task where a model needs to process the sentiments of users in live social media streams. For example, Chain of thought prompting might decompose the sentiment analysis task, while React Prompting enables the model to use external functions like sentiment analysis libraries or APIs, for a more complete analysis.

React and Chain of Thoughts Prompting in Action

Task 1: *Calculate when I need to leave home in Mumbai to reach Siddhivinayak Temple for the 6:00 AM aarti.*

Purpose: This task is intended to demonstrate how an LLM may deconstruct a problem and provide a step-by-step explanation of the reasoning behind it. Presenting the logic behind the response is meant to help the user comprehend the variables that go into deciding when to go.

Steps:

- **Think**: "I need to determine the travel time from my home in Andheri to Siddhivinayak Temple. I'll use a map or web search to get an accurate travel estimate."
- **Action**: Use Google Maps or a similar tool to search for "Travel time from Andheri to Siddhivinayak Temple."
- **Think**: "Since this is early in the morning, there might be unpredictable traffic or parking delays near the temple. I'll factor in an extra 15 minutes as buffer time for these variables."

- **Think**: "I also need to consider how early I should arrive at the temple to get a good spot for the 6:00 AM aarti. I'll look up recommended arrival times or check online experiences from other devotees.
- **Action**: Search online for "Recommended arrival time for Siddhivinayak Temple morning arti."

Result: "Devotees recommend arriving at least 30 minutes early to secure a good spot for the morning aarti."

Explanation: In this task, the LLM is asked to calculate when the user should leave home in Andheri, Mumbai, to reach Siddhivinayak Temple for the 6:00 AM aarti. The model breaks down the problem into smaller steps: first, it calculates the travel time from Andheri to the temple. Then, it considers additional factors like early morning traffic and potential parking delays, adding buffer time. The model also checks online for recommended arrival times, so the user knows how early to arrive at the temple to secure a spot. This example is used to guide the user through the reasoning process, explaining each step in detail.

Task 2: *Calculate when I need to leave home in Bengaluru to attend a conference at the India Habitat Centre, Delhi, starting at 10:00 AM.*

Purpose: This task asks the LLM to **perform** the same reasoning process as in Task 1 but with a focus on providing a direct solution to the user's problem. Instead of explaining the thought process step by step, the LLM uses its reasoning to calculate the answer.

Explanation: The user gives LLM a prompt that tells them how many hours they should leave Bengaluru to get to Delhi for the India Habitat Centre meeting, which starts at 10:00 am. In a similar manner, the LLM determines an estimate by first adjusting for delay and calibrating, then getting up, traveling, and reporting. Given the aforementioned considerations, the model is intended to provide the user with a precise departure time. In this instance, the LLM is providing a direct solution to the issue without elaborating on its methodology.

Few Example Scenarios for React Prompting

Example 1

As a simple example, let us suppose the model is computing the end of a live-streamed event. React Prompting allows the model to query the latest data that concerns the duration of the concerned events, allowing it to calculate an accurate end time.

Example 2

Imagine a language model that helps you schedule virtual meetings. From an externals/components perspective, React Prompting could autosuggest the model to use add-ons/third-party tools to check if members are able to make it, and automatically suggest meeting times.

Example 3

For instance, if an AI model is being trained to analyse market trends, React Prompting may allow the model to pull current information from external financial databases; this way, the model can take into account the latest market trends and economic indicators when making predictions.

Example 4

Imagine an AI assistant that would help users decide on a plan for their day. *e.g.*, an integration with external calendar APIs that lets the model give recommendations on-the-fly based on the user's schedule being updated in real-time.

Example 5

For instance, as a React Prompting-based framework, Lang chain could facilitate a data analytics scenario in which the model engages with external data points, conducts intricate analyses, and continuously updates its insights according to real-time data.

To sum up, React Prompting is a powerful method to turn large language models into dynamic problem solvers. Lead them to not just think through a process, but also to find a way to integrate external tools and put forth the groundwork for AI systems that go beyond text. These systems interact with their reality and tools in a way that makes them the most efficient systems known.

CONCLUSION

The chapter emphasizes how React Prompting and Chain of Thought Interaction can revolutionize conversational AI systems' capabilities. By integrating real-time external data into their processing, React Prompting helps large language models (LLMs) become more contextually aware and adaptive. This capability allows LLMs to generate more accurate, customized outcomes, thereby increasing their practicality and relevance. Conversely, Chain of Thought Interaction fosters a structured approach to problem-solving, enabling LLMs to break down complex challenges into manageable components, ultimately presenting users with coherent and well-reasoned solutions. By merging these frameworks, conversational AI systems are better equipped to deliver nuanced insights, more pertinent responses, and an enriched user experience. Practical applications highlighted in case studies—such as healthcare diagnostics, customer service optimization, and efficient scheduling—underscore the significant contributions of these methodologies. Looking forward, the integration of these sophisticated interaction techniques is poised to become instrumental in advancing AI's ability to navigate intricate inquiries, empower user decision-making, and facilitate more fluid, intuitive conversations.

REFERENCES

[1] M. Verma, S. Bhambri, and S. Kambhampati, "On the brittle foundations of react prompting for agentic large language models", May 22, 2024.
[http://dx.doi.org/10.48550/arXiv.2405.13966]

[2] S. Yao, "ReAct: Synergizing reasoning and acting in language models", Mar. 10, 2023.
[http://dx.doi.org/10.48550/arXiv.2210.03629]

[3] J. Chen, Z. Liu, X. Huang, C. Wu, Q. Liu, G. Jiang, Y. Pu, Y. Lei, X. Chen, X. Wang, K. Zheng, D. Lian, and E. Chen, "When large language models meet personalization: perspectives of challenges and opportunities", *World Wide Web (Bussum),* vol. 27, no. 4, p. 42, 2024.
[http://dx.doi.org/10.1007/s11280-024-01276-1]

[4] J. Wei, "Chain-of-thought prompting elicits reasoning in large language models", Jan. 10, 2023.
[http://dx.doi.org/10.48550/arXiv.2201.11903]

[5] L. Zequan, W. Longhao, and L. Xingsen, "The method of utilizing prompt engineering to train large language models for the intelligent expression of affair-elements", *Procedia Comput. Sci.,* vol. 242, pp. 1179-1184, 2024.
[http://dx.doi.org/10.1016/j.procs.2024.08.178]

[6] P. Sahoo, A.K. Singh, S. Saha, V. Jain, S. Mondal, and A. Chadha, "A systematic survey of prompt engineering in large language models: techniques and applications", Feb. 05, 2024.
[http://dx.doi.org/10.48550/arXiv.2402.07927]

[7] G.G. Lee, E. Latif, X. Wu, N. Liu, and X. Zhai, "Applying large language models and chain-o--thought for automatic scoring", *Computers and Education: Artificial Intelligence,* vol. 6, p. 100213, 2024.
[http://dx.doi.org/10.1016/j.caeai.2024.100213]

[8] Z. Zhang, A. Zhang, M. Li, and A. Smola, "Automatic chain of thought prompting in large language models", *International Conference on Learning Representations (ICLR),* 2022.
[http://dx.doi.org/10.48550/arXiv.2210.03493]

CHAPTER 8

Crafting Queries: Revealing the Mastery Behind Prompt Patterns

Abstract: This chapter covers the subtle art of query construction using unique prompt patterns in the context of large language models (LLMs). These patterns, which are known as strategic frameworks, have an impact on decision-making and user experiences that extend beyond linguistic triggers. The chapter explains how these frameworks can be used to create dynamic and interactive applications for a variety of industries, such as gaming, education, and corporate communication. For instance, gameplay patterns offer an engaging mechanism to captivate users through interactive challenges, fostering deeper learning and promoting problem-solving skills. Meta-language creation patterns enable more streamlined interactions with LLMs, providing users with efficient shorthand tools to handle intricate tasks. Similarly, the recipe pattern—structured through sequential steps addresses gaps in information, supporting users as they tackle complex problems. The semantic filter pattern further enhances the precision of responses by ensuring that outputs remain contextually accurate and relevant, filtering out extraneous or irrelevant details. Throughout the chapter, practical case studies and examples illuminate the application of these prompt patterns, demonstrating their transformative impact in real-world settings. Whether facilitating innovation in education, advancing operational strategies in business, or fostering creativity in gaming, these frameworks represent critical tools for leveraging the potential of LLMs effectively and innovatively.

Keywords: Dynamic problem solving, Gameplay patterns, Large Language Models (LLMs), Meta language creation, Prompt patterns, Semantic filters.

INTRODUCTION

The patterns prompt goes beyond the typical and frequently used language triggers, as it falls under the larger field of pattern recognition. As we continue this adventure, we find ourselves traversing a variety of landscapes since every design adds a unique thread to the intricate web of prompt-driven frameworks. Prompts are typically thought of as linguistic devices that are employed to elicit a specific response. Our tour, however, crosses these linguistic barriers and enters an unexplored area where prompt patterns affect decision-making and user experience. In the realm of gaming, game-play patterns are more than just words;

Sumit Tripathi

they influence gameplay dynamics and mechanics to create engrossing, immersive experiences [1]. Furthermore, the production patterns of the meta language direct elegantly structured processes, not only in the kitchen but in every sequential operation. Building languages that define and influence other languages is what the meta-language development patterns introduce us to.

This meta-level investigation shows how communication paradigms are set up to express intricate relationships and ideas. Tail generation patterns focus on flexibility and responsiveness in producing relevant material and deal with the dynamic development of information or content that expands from an existing dataset. In the field of information retrieval and processing, semantic filter patterns sort information on the basis of context and relevance to promote semantic understanding in retrieval [2]. Because interface design guides the user through a series of choices and related actions, menu action patterns for the user interface specify actions to present from menus and require investigating the potential effects of interface design on how a user interacts.

GAMEPLAY PATTERNS

This is an exploration of the world of gaming, where the art of prompt engineering takes the centre stage as a fundamental element in crafting interactive adventures across digital landscapes. Here, prompt engineering within gameplay patterns symbolizes a higher-level amalgamation of creativity and strategic design — each prompt acting as a strategic lever, guiding player decision-making and shaping the trajectory of immersive narratives. At its heart, prompt engineering is the art of crafting prompts that guide players through an exciting and immersive experience. These prompts become the sparks that compel reactions, decisions, and actions that ultimately shape the trajectory of a story within a game. Not just words to the wise, these prompts serve as tactical devices finely tuned to elicit specific feelings, shape player behavior, and foster a sense of dominion over the digital landscape. Drive ambitions to meet enhanced patterns of gameplay through prompt engineering [3]. Prompt engineering will help define the shapes of these patterns and, in turn, affect exploration, competition, solving puzzles, cooperation, etc. From the first word to the last, each prompt is a stroke of a brush on a canvas of player engagement, making a difference not only to game mechanics, but to the feelings that it leaves with you as you partake in the game. In this exploration, we seek to reveal the hidden artistry behind these prompts, the psychology that propels them, and the design that brings a prompt to life to create an experience that leaves players with an organic feeling of connection to the digital reality being built through their actions [4].

What is a Gameplay Pattern?

The Gameplay Pattern essentially leverages the capabilities of large language models such as ChatGPT to play the role of the "game master" in the learning process. At its core, it is about transforming learning into a game in which the model sets the rules and challenges. From here, users work through these challenges, not only learning the material more deeply but also delighting in the fun of interactive, rewarding learning.

Example 1: Prompt Engineering Challenge

Setting the Stage

For example, suppose a user wants to learn prompt engineering, an important skill for gaining an interest in large language models.

The Challenge

The game master, ChatGPT, gives a challenge: "Write a program that takes a list of numbers as input and returns whether the list contains any duplicate elements. If duplicates are present, return 'yes'; otherwise, state 'no duplicate found'."

Prompt Engineering

The user needs to create a prompt to ask ChatGPT to solve this task. Their tools serve as few-shot examples, nudging the model toward a specific output format. The objective of the user is to prompt adeptly and elicit correct responses.

Game Progression

A prompt is given to ChatGPT, and it provides an output. The user evaluates the response, not only for correctness, but also for how well their prompt succeeded in conveying the task. The challenge structure creates an iteratively repetitive challenge by default, while everything else ends up honing the user's prompt engineering skills.

The Gameplay Pattern has the unique feature to inject logic or programming elements into the challenges. With the addition of reasoning elements, the game becomes more than just a leisurely activity; it becomes an answer to complex problems, promoting problem-solving skills through the chosen topic.

Example 2: Sentence Analysis Challenge

Setting the Stage

Think of a reader who gets excited about sentence analysis (a linguistic and logical challenge!)

The Challenge

Examples usage: Given a sentence, count the number of words and return the result in that format, "The sentence contains X words" where X is the number of words.

Prompt Engineering

A template pattern is used by the user as a great way to outline the structure of the output. The task of ChatGPT is to produce a prompt that counts the words in a sentence according to the designated system.

Game Progression

ChatGPT replies with a challenge-specific prompt. This loss is evaluated by the user, and keeping the correct format is a top priority. The challenge both sharpens the prompt, promotes engineering precision and develops logical problem-solving.

Use of Training Data for Rich Content

The Gameplay Pattern is powerful because it leverages huge amounts of training data imbued by large language models. It uses this vast knowledge to arbitrarily create challenges that maintain diversity and content in an entertaining and instructional gaming experience.

Leap Year Determiner Game

Setting the Stage

Consider a user who is interested in how leap years are calculated and wants to learn more in a dynamic way.

The Challenge

Input: You are given a date in the format yyyy, mm, dd, and your task is to determine if the year is a leap year or not. Cmd+F to read the result, whether it is or it is not a leap year.

Prompt Engineering

The user uses a few-shot examples, asking ChatGPT to find leap years without requiring source code.

Game Progression

For the given date, ChatGPT understands and solves leap year tasks. In addition to testing the effectiveness of the user prompts, it further enhances their challenge design skills and understanding of leap-year determination.

Creating Games for Specific Prompt Patterns

When users specialize in other prompt pattern categories, the adaptability of the Gameplay Pattern is evident. Through incorporating prompt patterns characteristic of specific papers or domains, users may customize games to analyse leading areas to gain insight into the ways to advance in predetermined areas.

For Instance: Recipe Prompt Challenge

Setting the Stage

Imagine a user filters the gameplay down to revolve around one specific prompt pattern—like the recipe prompt pattern.

The Challenge

"Write a prompt where you ask me to make a list for you on how to put together a basic wooden bookshelf." The prompt needs to help the model deliver an explicit sequence of events for assembly.

Prompt Engineering

Based on the recipe prompt pattern, the user defines the context and bounds. ChatGPT is given the instructions to create a prompt for you to assemble a bookshelf.

Game Progression

ChatGPT replies with prompts that direct the assembly process. It becomes a matter for the user to assess which clusters of pill responses are clear and complete, and to learn how to craft prompts as much as possible from the experience of staying in the dish recipe prompt pattern.

The Gameplay Pattern is a texture that is of great help in the journey to learning and honing skills. Users can interact with large language models at varying levels of playfulness and unpredictability, facilitating learning in an engaging way. The aforementioned examples illustrate the versatility of this pattern; it is effective for logical problem-solving, prompt-based problem-solving, and extensive knowledge repositories. Have fun with it, try things out, and explore the possibilities of the Gameplay Pattern.

Example: Gamifying People, Games: A Feasibility Study of Implementing Game Play Patterns in Corporate Training

Introduction

One particular implementation is the strategy to integrate gameplay to improve employee training and development.

Keywords: Game play patterns, Training, Gamification, Corporate enterprises, Case study.

Objective

The focus was chiefly on enhancing employee engagement and ensuring better retention of training content along with the effectiveness of overall corporate training programs.

Design and Implementation

The game designers worked alongside subject matter experts to develop a gamified training platform that used effective patterns of gameplay.

Levels of Progressive Learning

The course content was divided into progressive levels, where each level represented distinct business operations. As developers progressed through the levels, they would unlock new levels of challenge, as well as insights into the workings of the company at large.

Reward and Recognition

To motivate employees to complete modules, master specific domain skills, and achieving milestones, achievements, and badges were introduced. Not only was it positive reinforcement, but it helped create a sense of healthy competition among employees.

Simulated Workplace

The game had realistic business scenarios, offering employees a platform to utilize their learned theories in simulated real-world situations. It taught them practical skills for a world with which they would often practice Montessori principles.

Multiplayer challenges were included, promoting teamwork and communication. This ingrained a sense of camaraderie amongst the employees, where it was clear that they are a teamthat is the sole reason for achieving the corporate objectives. As a result, we witnessed higher productivity, and, due to a healthier workplace atmosphere, interpersonal relations in the workplace reported no gossip among colleagues.

Results

The corporate training program gave way to implementing gameplay patterns that translated to real benefits:

More Engagement: Employees showed greater engagement with the training content, boosted by the interactive and competitive aspects of the game play patterns.

Gamification Positive Impact on Training Engagement and Performance: Enhanced Knowledge Retention: Employees were more engaged in the learning process by applying concepts and resolving challenges in the virtual business setting, resulting in improved knowledge retention of the training materials.

Increased Team Dynamics: Team challenges improved team dynamics, encouraging team members from different departments to work together and communicate more.

The success of "BizQuest" showed how well game-play patterns can work in the business domain for employee education. This gamified approach not only made the process fun but also translated into improved engagement, knowledge retention, and team dynamics. The following case study showcases how gameplay patterns can be used to turn a mundane corporate training into a gamified experience that provides an effective learning experience.

META LANGUAGE CREATION PATTERN

A key component of follow-up, as the field of language model interfacing develops, is efficient communication. A unique and effective approach to enhancing the simplicity and clarity of communication with large language models is the Meta Language Creation Pattern. In this section, we explore the intricate details of the Meta Language Creation Pattern, examining its potential uses and methods [5]. The Meta Language Creation Pattern is not simply the development of a language, it is a strategy to facilitate the idea/thought exchange. Using meta-language — language whose subject matter is language, users can specifically model and control the behaviour of language models [6]. ChatGPT, however, operates using a fixed pattern that goes beyond the classic conversational form and gives users more direct control of how they want to interact with the AI.

Specialized (Domain Specific) Languages

There is a tendency to spend more time and energy thinking about the exchange of ideas than on the exchange itself. Whether through words, sound, or movement, we do not separate from communication, and so in complex literal and metaphorical landscapes, we are increasingly becoming the messengers that need to be trusted. Navigating these complex landscapes requires a significant skillset, particularly the capacity to convey ideas, communicate information, and react to adversity. In areas of precision and efficiency, it is inevitable that specialized forms of language develop that convey meaning as directly and succinctly as possible. SKIP:16 In real-life examples, if you read this at Nashville emergency responders, KEEPING staying from specialized languages. For example, in time-sensitive medical situations, these professionals may resort to shorthand, highlighting the necessity of concise, specialized communication in medical emergencies. This new awareness emphasizes the importance of customized communication tools in situations where understanding takes precedence over information, common in stressful environments where speed is key, as was the case when discussing this study in relation to emergency care.

Recognizing the Meta Language creation Template

Meta has pioneered the Language Creation Pattern, which offers an entirely new paradigm of allowing users to create and train separate languages over large language models. In traditional communication, we may need to explain using full English sentences, but there are situations where we can do so in a more compact, specialized way. Basically, this pattern is analogous to a few-shot examples but almost a long-shortcut version. It allows you to share little chunks of information quickly and accurately — on a whole new level of personalization when it comes to everyday language use. One of the reasons you will see such a leap in performance, both in terms of efficiency and effectiveness, is the ability to establish a shorthand with a predefined meaning within the context of that Meta Language Creation Pattern, which translates into a drastic improvement in your use case.

Example 1: A Trip Planning Application — Basic Notation

For a small example to demonstrate how the Meta Language Creation Pattern works in practice, let us take a trip planning story: Users shall then use short notation to avoid battling against verbose descriptions. So, for instance, entering "Nashville, zero" could mean avoid Nashville, whereas "Dallas, one arrow Grandberry Texas, four" could convey a particular travel route and information on how long you plan to stay in the locations. This primitive notational scheme is a basis for building a more elaborate language.

Example 2: Trip Planning Application — Notation ++

Continuing with the trip planning example, say you have a more complex statement: "Goa to Mumbai, three days, Pune, one day, Nashik, one day." This complex line summarizes a detailed itinerary. The user does not just input words; they teach the language to the large language model! It has a learning step, where you can provide samples such as this in extended forms, and by their decomposition , it closes the gap between the user and the model. In this way, the Meta Language Creation Pattern allows for the conveyance of complexity with precision between any number of axes to integrate.

Making and Teaching the Language

The Meta Language Creation Pattern primarily focuses on the user's fluency in the language that the model needs to learn. This is more than simply spitting out some phrases; it requires full translations along with extensive context. For example, take this: "Nashville, zero." In order to successfully convey the intended meaning, the user needs to provide a complete translation, such as: "I mean my route from Nashville goes to Memphis, and I will spend three days in Nashville, and two days in Memphis." This painstakingly detailed explanation is not just a formality; it is the key ingredient for ensuring the correct interpretation of the language model. The level of accuracy and clarity used when teaching the language is a big part. They allow the model to grasp and produce contextually appropriate replies based on the user's abbreviated entries. In fact, in a travel-planning scenario, a user might present the model with specific terms related to travel preferences, like "NYC, hotel, Fri-Sun." Such shorthand could be painstakingly parsed in the teaching phase to indicate that, for the aforementioned time span from Friday to Sunday, the user would like hotel accommodation together in New York City. This teaches the language model a finer understanding of the intent behind the input, allowing it to produce more accurate outputs.

Using the Meta Language for Trip Planning

After this, as soon as users include the language in their conversation, they can instantly fill in short-answer statements that give the large language model a simple code to understand and turn into itineraries. Their true effectiveness and accuracy are revealed, particularly for repetitive or complex tasks. For example, imagine a user teaching the language model a set of commands for scheduling meetings. Then, the model understands and outputs the itinerary by simply having the input condensed, for example, instead of saying "Create a meeting with Team A on Monday at 2 PM", Beyond rote activities, the Meta Language Creation Pattern has the potential to transform interactions. It metamorphoses, simplifying and channelling mundane interactions into seamless, effective processes. For example, in a business scenario, the user could use the pattern to simplify complex project management instructions. Such complex details can be expressed in a much simpler, shorter format, such as "Start Project X, give updates every Friday," and the intelligent system can then understand the task and fulfil the requirements quickly, saving the user a great deal of time and effort. This translates detailed instructions into crisp language and, by doing so, allows users to experience a new dimension of interaction with the language model, which not only helps with productivity but also improves human-to-language model communication. This is most notably seen in complex data analysis tasks, where the end user can specify a brief query, and the language model — fully trained to understand complex input textprovides structured analysis without requiring the user to provide every field in the input section.

Pros and Cons

These advantages are primarily efficiency and precision-oriented, as outlined by the Meta Language Creation Pattern. Any organization can use this concept internally to navigate the cultural catch-up process by making sure the music is kept in sync. But it is essential to instruct users on how to use the language appropriately to eliminate vagueness and promote the correct understanding. It is important to be specific, but you do not want to be too specific either.

Introducing a new pattern of language creation at Meta. As an evolutionary step in the realm of natural language interaction, this pattern simultaneously serves as a powerful method for generating and teaching language, as well as providing its users a doorway to the vast abilities included within the architecture of large language models. Intelligent and agile handling of the complex nuances of creating and teaching language allows people and organizations to unlock a wide array of opportunities by interacting with these sophisticated linguistic engines. The Meta Language Creation Pattern is a masterclass in exploring these techniques, which enable users to exploit the full potential of large language models.

Case Study

Transforming the Face of Business Communication: A Case Study on the Implementation of Meta Language Creation Pattern

Introduction

The Meta Language Creating Pattern has become a disruptive force in the world of business communication. In this case study, we will explore how a global marketing firm called "GlobalCom" successfully adopted the Meta Language Creation Pattern and examine its effect on efficient communication and collaboration within the organization.

Objective

The objective was to create a unified platform for more effective communication, better understanding between diverse teams, and to foster faster decision-making within the complexity of GlobalCom's business.

Implementation

The communication transformation at GlobalCom was driven by the use of the Meta Language Creation Pattern:

META Language Creation Pattern: The META Language Creation Pattern was devised to provide customized communication tailored to the vocabulary and communication styles used within GlobalCom's niche. The system enabled personnel to communicate complex information simply and in a consistent format.

Integration and Training: An in-depth training plan was created to train employees in the Meta Language Creation Pattern. The sessions covered real-life use cases with hands-on experience for smooth adoption into everyday communication practices.

Cross-Functional Collaboration type: The Meta Language Creation Pattern promoted cross-functional collaboration by defining a common language across diverse teams. More insightful about popular and neglected products — Marketing, sales, and creative departments could now communicate more effectively, reducing misunderstanding and increasing overall productivity.

Streamlined Decision-Making: The pattern enabled faster decision-making processes. Rather than lengthy discussions, teams could share critical information quickly, allowing leadership to make informed decisions more quickly.

Results

There were major benefits to GlobalCom through using the Meta Language Creation Pattern. The Meta Language Creation Pattern resulted in an increased efficiency of communication, where less time was utilized in decoding long-winded messages, and staff time could now be used on strategic initiatives.

Improved Collaboration: Teams began to collaborate significantly better through cross-functionality, as they were able to communicate naturally using the standardized language, which often broke silos and improved teamwork.

Faster Decision-Making: The simplified communication process enabled GlobalCom to react more quickly to market shifts and seize new opportunities.

Conclusion

Towards the end of the article, you will see an example of how GlobalCom implemented the Meta Language Creation Pattern. Within a global marketing firm, the Meta Language Creation Pattern served as a lever for integrating a way of life by creating a rapid decision-making process across all layers of the organization. This case study highlights the META language creation pattern's potential for revolutionizing ways of communicating and enabling agility in a business context.

RECIPE PATTERN

When dealing with problem-solving on the land of large language models, most of your time will be spent working around partial solutions. The primary obstacle is filling in the gaps as if putting together a puzzle or writing a recipe that involves a number of steps to reach a desired objective. This is also where the Recipe Pattern comes into play, serving as a powerful technique that allows users to leverage the power of large language models to bridge the gaps between information [7]. The Recipe Pattern establishes an affordance that allows users to navigate the complexity of the problems they are solving by asking LLMs for help. It walks through the nuances of the Recipe Pattern, a versatile tool with utility across domains, revealing the magic within the information haze. Essentially, the Recipe Pattern enables the transformation of data through its relatively straightforward structure, using large language models. It allows users to build upon their problem-solving capabilities and produce holistic solutions from even just partial snapshots of data [8]. You learn the nuances of which situations are particularly well-suited to the Recipe Pattern, including how to walk users through the process of writing step-by-step instructions, methodologies, or action plans. In addition, the chapter highlights the versatility of the Recipe Pattern, demonstrating its application in everything from technical problem-solving to creative ideation. It explains how users can make the most of large models' inherent knowledge and language understanding in order to become more efficient and effective problem solvers.

So the Recipe Pattern basically brings broader thoughts, back to the stage of how we should think about problem-solving with LLMs. This chapter is like an umbrella, providing users with the background and knowledge to understand and implement the Recipe Pattern, and how they will transform their views and thoughts when dealing with difficulties in different walks of life.

The Nature of Recipe Pattern

The Recipe Pattern is strictly the link between what we know and what we do not know. It hones our ability to build a rigid-to-follow recipe, a clear series of steps to take or things to get. At the same time, it leaves the remainder of the process and the filling in of all the missing pieces to the almost limitless potential of a large language model. When our goal is more general but we do not necessarily possess all the particulars to achieve it, this collaborative strategy can be extremely effective.

It is like having a broad goal or a pain point, but maybe not being able to clearly state exactly what you need to do or build to get there. This is where the Recipe Pattern comes to the rescue, as a facilitator, based on the fact that we can give an initial mining frame. The large language model fills in the gaps by injecting the missing pieces into this framework, which serves as our structure for the known elements. Such synergy leads to exhaustive, well-fleshed-out solutions that take an abstract/missing concept and make it well-defined and workable. The Recipe Pattern accelerates and doubles down on the best of both human input and machine intelligence. That recognizes our ability to sketch the larger outlines of a problem or task and partners with the text model's ability to fill in the fine-grained details. This two-pronged strategy is especially helpful for objectives that require us to embrace a broad overall vision with a bit of granularity in the details to make that vision real.

Example 1: Trip Planning Application – Introducing a New Feature

Let us return to the well-worn ground of the trip-planning application and see how the Recipe Pattern might improve the engagement for this user. Let us consider a situation where the user wants a complete list of stops between their source and destination but only knows their source and destination. Using the Recipe Pattern, the user can, in fact, accurately express this remainder-less fact: "Nashville, zero...arrow...Fairhope, Alabama, two." This coaxes the model into filling in the blanks with plausible drop-off points, such as Birmingham and Montgomery, naturally stitching together a robust itinerary.

Example 2: Extending the Complexity — Los Angeles to New York

To demonstrate how versatile the Recipe Pattern is, imagine a situation where the user wants to take a road trip from Los Angeles to New York, but they are not sure what stops they will make along the way. Using a more loosey-goosey phrasing like, "L.A....dot dot dot...New York" cues the model to be okay with many stops. Up until that date, the model interprets this vagueness as a suggestion of multiple target locations to allow for a more diverse journey.

Recipe Patterns in Conjunction with Meta Language Creation

When the Meta Language Creation Pattern meets the Recipe Pattern, a very powerful synergy is produced. Users do more than teach the model a compressed language; they employ this language, stretching it, bending it, to traverse, suit, and perform whole complex functions. This chapter examines how these patterns work together to promote efficient user communication and complex task completion. This synthesis enables users to create a shorthand for their conversations and also to serve as a tool for properly building up and executing complex processes and recipes.

Application of Recipe Pattern in Different Domains

The concept of a "Recipe Pattern" goes beyond trip planning, being applicable to different domains. People could leverage it for solving, planning, and stimulating creative ideation. The ability to ask for help solving hard problems through the provision of partial information greatly expands its applicability to a variety of situations. This versatility reinforces the wide array of use cases for the Recipe Pattern, providing a feature that can serve users across sectors and disciplines with improved efficiency and effectiveness of execution.

Considerations and Best Practices

The Recipe Pattern offers an agile solution, though it requires users to be judicious in articulating their goals and suggesting next steps. How to implement well-defined placeholders or prompts in a human-like text? Demonstrating clear feedback to the model helps the model produce accurate outputs and identifies relevant concepts. Finding that balance is important: providing enough specificity to guide the model while maintaining enough open-endedness so the solution can be solved in a unique way.

Why Recipe Pattern? The Recipe Pattern is an indispensable tool for collaborative problem-solving in language model interactions. In this chapter, a technique is presented to help transform only partial 'knowledge' provided by the user into 'actionable solutions' by seamlessly embedding user-provided frameworks into model-generated content. As a tutorial, it methodically weaves through the layers of the Recipe Pattern, equipping users with the tools to effectively utilise it across a broad spectrum of use cases. Lino is a skilled synthesizer of diverse perspectives, collaborating with personas such as scientists, policymakers, business leaders, and educators to consolidate expertise to address complex challenges for individuals, organizations, and nations in using fragmented information to achieve actionable results.

Recipe Pattern: A Case Study in Improving Product Development

Introduction

The project management tool developed for product development is designed to streamline diverse tasks and processes across seemingly unending activities. In this section, we present a case study from a software development company, "TechSprint," that details how the Recipe Pattern was applied to improve their product development processes.

Objective

The objective was to foster better collaboration amongst cross-functional teams, streamline communication, and speed up the product development life cycle.

Implementation

TechSprint knew that the Recipe Pattern would keep the development teams working together and speaking the same language. The implementation included the following major components:

Structured Task Assignments: Each project acts as a recipe with the various tasks representing the ingredients. The Recipe Pattern enabled teams to describe the steps they knew, while allowing the language model to help fill in gaps or make suggestions.

Real-time Collaboration: The Recipe Pattern enabled team members to share their expertise and provide insights into the project recipe as it developed. By working together, we improved the quality of project planning and execution.

Challenge: The problem is incorporating it into Agile development processes. It enabled teams to rapidly iterate on the recipe in response to changing requirements, facilitating an agile, responsive development approach.

Results

TechSprint`s use of the Recipe Pattern gave a lot of positive results:

Enhanced Collaboration: Teams across departments were able to work together more effectively. The Recipe Pattern is a way to extract a common language and structure to describe and plan our shared work, promoting clarity and minimizing miscommunication.

Faster-To-Market By Process: The process, enabled by Recipe Pattern, resulted in a shorter product development life cycle. Having an option to quickly create detailed project plans made it feasible for teams to participate in a smarter manner and then make innovative things happen.

Quality Improvement: This collaboration (Recipe Pattern) ultimately led to more optimal and complete project planning stages. This helped teams leverage diverse expertise, leading to higher-quality outputs.

Conclusion

Overall, the Recipe Pattern used at TechSprint proves to be an effective way to add structure to collaboration and communication, and has found ways to improve the overall efficiency going through product development. The Recipe Pattern demonstrated how a structured framework could facilitate generative responses using content produced by a model, resulting in a constructive blend of partial knowledge and actionable interpretation. And finally, this case illustrates how the Recipe Pattern, when used in the right way, can have a positive impact on product management by bringing systems thinking and usability to the forefront, thus developing a better product much faster in a competitive and dynamic market.

TAIL GENERATION PATTERN

In the field of sustained engagements with large language models, a recurring issue tends to arise—something known as forgetting, where models forget rules and goals set out at the outset of a conversation as it goes on. Addressing this problem and ensuring continuous and sustained conversation, the "Tail Generation Pattern" offers an innovative concept. This approach involves structurally tacking on a relevant "tail" to the end of whatever the model's inputs are, reminding the model of the current endeavour and its principles along the way [9]. By seamlessly incorporating this innovative technique, developers intend to enhance the model's ability to follow user instructions, leading to smoother, more on-topic dialogue. In this introduction, we delve into how we can leverage the Tail Generation Pattern to alleviate the problem of model forgetfulness during a long conversation, and how this could help improve the overall coherence and effectiveness of AI interactions.

Tail Generation Importance

The Tail Generation will require some detailed implementation since the central idea of the Tail Generation Pattern is to strengthen the contextual capabilities of the model as a conversation progresses [10]. This idea revolves around offering a subtle yet constant reminder about the rules, goals, or general context of the current discussion. Tacked on at the end of the model output, this little gem is a straight-up warning, like the orderly standing in front of the grand pansion saying, "ok, you don't have your gloves on, but just don't rub off that glitter you worked so hard to get on in the first place." Its main job is coherence, making sure that the model knows how to respond throughout longer conversations, in particular. This decision to place the reminder at the end of the model output is a powerful tactic in the Tail Generation Pattern. In other words, developers play with the recency effect, an aspect of the model that creates a bias that weighs the last batch of data in a conversation more than the previous ones. By positioning the reminder in this manner, it becomes a prompt for the model to remember the rules, objectives, or contextual information defined over the course of an ongoing conversation, and to orient towards them as a part of it.

Align Tail Generation with Complementary Strategies: Ask-for-Input Patterns and Other Approaches

Integrating the Tail Generation Pattern with other conversational strategies maximizes its effectiveness. We now describe the interrelations among the Tail Generation Pattern, the Alternative Approaches Pattern, and the Ask-for-Input Pattern. These strategies involving step-by-step interaction allow the model to swim through tasks in a smooth way, taking steps in the conversational flow to refocus on different targets. The Tail Generation Pattern is an approach in which the system adds reminders to the end of the model output to prevent it from forgetting rules, goals, or context, while the Tail Generation Pattern represents the system as a constant guide and reminder to the model, ensuring it always follows the rules. The Alternative Approaches Pattern adds depth to the conversation by encouraging the model to produce multiple formats or takes, while the Tail Generation Pattern ensures that these alternatives stay within the boundaries of what is palatable to the user. The Ask-for-Input Pattern is a way of encouraging dialogue with the user to gather more information on what the user is thinking about. A sample scenario demonstrates how each of the concepts integrates into a programming task where the Tail Generation Pattern establishes context, the Alternative Approaches Pattern offers variety in code generation, and the Ask-fo--Input Pattern requests a more refined query. Such orchestrated flow enables us to smoothly move between conversations with varying objectives that align with user input, leading to more engaging, user-centric interactions that dynamically adjust to changing dialogue patterns.

Example: Prompt Engineering Designer

Tail generator pattern is one of the most useful patterns in the case of prompt engineering, wherein the task is to make a model generate a prompt on a loop. The self-updating loop is created by building a tail that specifically asks for the next input for prompt generation. As a result, this reinforces the task repeatedly, reducing the risk that the model will deviate too far from the defined rules and objectives.

Strategic Application for Extended Interactions

The Tail Generation Pattern is best suited for long-lived interactions. Be it assigning rules to a model's code or using guiding principles for a complex task, the tail is a constant anchor. It gathers critical information and regularly reminds the model of the prearranged goals to maintain engagement and coherence.

Tail Content writes themselves (rules/context/instructions)

Tail content does not have to follow a strict format. Developers can customize the tail to regain rules, provide context or information, or ask for details based on specific needs. Tail Generation Pattern is flexible, which allows developers to adjust it according to different conversational scenarios and goals.

The Tail Generation Pattern helps create cognitive continuity and is an important strategy for learning how to talk to large language models. By positioning it at the end of the model's output, it ensures the information can be properly integrated, reducing forgetting. Tail generation enables the application developers to operate beyond those synthetic sentence patterns, among trees of large language models to produce meaningful and coherent responses.

Usage: Tail in Summary of Research and Reinforcement of User Instructions

User Query: "Tell me about recent developments in artificial intelligence with an emphasis on progress in natural language processing."

Model Response: The new developments in AI, especially in natural language processing, contribute significantly to the recent growth of transformer-based models. These kinds of models (for example, GPT-4) have shown astonishing power in language understanding and generation. In addition, advancements in transfer learning approaches have laid the foundation for more efficient and successful text predictive systems."

Tail Generation: "Keep mentioning advances in natural language processing in later responses."

Explanation: As an example of one of these methods, the Tail Generation Pattern is used to hone in on the user's particular instruction to put emphasis on breakthroughs in natural language processing. Thus, if the appended tail presents the supplementary instruction, it reminds the model to mention proposed information in further responses, hence allowing it to be coherent with the request made by the user.

Case Study: How Tail Generation Pattern Enhances Customer Support Interaction

Background

Challenge: A well-versed e-commerce platform wanted to enhance its customer support conversations using a smart AI language model. The main difficulty was to elicit different yet contextually relevant responses during the long chat with clients, while also adhering to the company's business rules and defined goals.

Objective: The objective was to utilize the Tail Generation Pattern to enhance continuity and coherence in customer support conversations. Accordingly, the focus was on integrating this pattern into the existing AI framework by supplementing business-specific guidelines, presenting users with targeted support interfaces, and seamlessly transitioning between different customer queries.

Implementation

User Query Initiation:

User: "I have a problem with my latest order. Can you help me track it?"

Initial Model Response:

The model generates a response addressing the order tracking query and appending a tail.

"Certainly! I get the need to track your order. Here is the current status. Feel free to ask for any further help you need."

Tail Generation Pattern in Action:

Tailor: Make sure every response reflects our commitment to the customer and to resolution in a timely fashion

User Follow-up Query:

User: "Can you also tell me about the return process?

Response Model with Tail Guidance:

Return instruction inquiries about the information you should send for returning the items.

"Absolutely! Please see our returns process in depth here. If there's anything particular you want to know, please ask. We wish you to have a hassle-free experience."

Tail Continuity

Tail: "If there are any concerns, then be sure to have a customer-first tone and be proactive to resolve)"

Results

The customer support interactions, implemented with the Tail Generation Pattern, had several positive outcomes:

A Constant Customer-Oriented Approach: Tail-Based answers reinforced a sound customer central tone, always focusing the user type experience.

Following Business Guidelines: The tail served as a reminder of the company-specific rules governing that business, so the AI model could follow company policy and answer user questions in a way the company would approve of.

Smooth Transitions and Continuity of Tasks: Thanks to the Tail Generation Pattern, each user query was processed in a standard way from start to end. From tracking orders to handling returns, the model consistently maintained context and relevance.

Increased User Satisfaction: Users were happier with tailored, coherent responses, leading to higher satisfaction rates. The customized support and compliance with corporate policies resulted in a great customer experience.

Conclusion

The customer support interactions of the e-commerce platform were effectively improved using the Tail Generation Pattern, enabling them to facilitate continuity, coherence, and a user-centric approach. This case study illustrates the use of the Tail Generation Pattern in the context of a business case and can serve as a useful guide to remain contextually relevant, follow guidelines and offer the user a more satisfying experience.

MENU ACTION PATTERN

As a new pattern for prompts, the Menu Actions Pattern emerged within the paradigm of commonly used software, whose user interface patterns typically unfold through menus of structured actions. This method allows prompt engineers to present a precise, organized menu of actions in a chat, adding pre-defined activities that are initiated upon specific phrases in the input [2]. This is a big step in conversational experience design that enables prompt engineers to create interactive menus where users can explore options similar to navigating through a software interface. The table above depicts this structured menu, where clear paths are created for users through actions, triggers, and instructions they can use to start a task using natural language. To illustrate, a user could simply issue a command, such as "Get information about [topic]," and the model would perform the task and return relevant results. The Menu Actions Pattern can be tailored to any context, and its versatility enables it to improve user-friendly interactions and transform the communication dynamics in conversational AI across different software.

Building a Prompt Menu: Actions and Definitions

This is a well-engineered syntax for additional clarification on how to perform certain tasks in the flow. This regulated syntax includes a command—like "write" — that is followed by placeholders for bullet points and the number of paragraphs. By designing it in this specific format, it is given a model and a guidebook for understanding and performing predefined tasks in response to user input. The syntax uses placeholders, which enable context-specific responses, thus allowing the model to generate the request a user is asking about. By employing keywords and placeholders in this pattern, we can create a structure that ensures the model continues to adhere to the specified action guidelines in a reactive, user-oriented way.

Syntax and Structure: Navigating the Menu

In a practical enactment of the Menu Actions Pattern, imagine a user collaborating with an AI language model in a content-generation setting. A user gives the model a command: "Fill in key points in the outline for our upcoming presentation." Within the context of the Menu Actions Pattern, the model has a fixed menu to refer back to, so it knows that this prompt is asking to "elaborate" on certain points. Once the user defines the structure of what the response should look like by using the syntax of the pattern, they can further tweak their instruction by referencing a specific bullet or paragraph number. For example, the user might say, "Elaborate on point two of the outline." This is a declaration for the AI, which tells it to add more information on each of those points. There is another action on the menu: "write." For example, you could smoothly instruct the model with a prompt like, "Create a summary for the introduction. Will the model generate the code based on what the user specifies? What does the user want from the interface? How to use it?

By using a given menu paired with the syntactical paradigm, a user can smoothly direct the model to take different actions, creating a cooperative, responsive conversational dynamic. The sheer elegance of the Menu Actions Pattern lies in its ability to quickly turn a dialogue into an animated, user-level experience. With this pattern's capabilities, users can perform established actions with ease, negating the need for colourful or lengthy prompts. This transmutational nature gives the interaction a direction of stylization; suddenly, prompts do not merely serve as requests but as a codex that the model interprets and executes. With the user experience being more streamlined, it becomes more intuitive and responsive, as the model beautifully understands and engages with nuanced requests. With the help of the Menu Actions Pattern, this level of interactivity creates an experience that leaves users smiling and marks a strong progressive step towards naturalistic conversations, seamlessly exercising the flow and individually addressing user intent. In this sense, it also gives a pretty good level of intelligence in the way that the model treats the prompts according to the Menu Actions Pattern. This unauthorized job is impressive, and even when the user makes spelling mistakes or deviates slightly from the required syntax, the model still understands their intention very well. It is this flexibility that is a testament to how well-designed this pattern is and to how it greatly improves the quality of the user experience. This builds a bridge between user input and desired outcomes, allowing the model to accurately process the request and generate appropriate responses without getting confused by slight differences in phrasing or wording. So all this flexibility makes the Menu Actions Pattern as a whole quite resilient and user-friendly with respect to the different ways instructions could be expressed by the user.

The Menu Actions Pattern serves as a valuable knowledge-sharing tool in organizational settings. Prompt engineers can outline a series of actions for a set of common phrases and share them in a standardized way across teams as a pattern. Such a systematic approach not only enhances efficiency by helping streamline the process of creating interactive prompts but also ensures that best practices are consistently codified and applied across the organization. With a unified menu of actions, teams can better align across different workflows, making it easier to collaborate and providing a smoother conversational experience. It is essentially a standard way to store the common knowledge that prompt engineers can use to refer to predefined actions that have been shown to work. Thus, the Menu Actions Pattern serves as a means of sharing knowledge, allowing teams to learn from each other and to readily access a rich set of standardized actions. Not only does this speed up the development of conversational interactions, but it also gives a feeling of consistency and reliability when following best practices across the various teams within the organization.

With the Menu Actions Pattern, prompt engineers have what they need to make swift work of prompt development. By allowing engineers to create their own menu of pre-determined actions, the process moves more quickly, and the conversation is more helpful and less time-consuming. Additionally, the menu pattern helps facilitate teamwork; professionals from different disciplines can design menus that help their fellow team members work more quickly and in unison. The result is a prompt development pipeline that is not only more efficient but also more beneficial to all parties involved. In a sense, this pattern represents the culmination of the prompt, turning it from a one-way communication element into a more dynamic and beneficial set of instructions. Hence, the primary qualities of the pattern are efficiency, teamwork, and communication, which help to bring a more engaging conversation with the assistant closer.

Case Study Example: An Example of Data Usage in an Encounter

Background

The subject was a technology company that focused on collaborative software development, and wanted to streamline communications and increase the efficiency of project-related discussions. The Menu Actions Pattern is implemented to elicit a structured and interactive flow of project tasks and updates within the organization.

Objective

The ultimate goal was to use the Menu Actions Pattern to compose a set of project collaboration actions that were consistent. This meant setting up specific actions, such as assigning tasks, updating progress, or requesting feedback, to keep project conversations more streamlined and organized.

Implementation: Collaboratively Building a Series Menu

Prompt engineers established a menu of common actions that teams take to collaborate on a project (e.g., "Assign Task," "Provide Update," and "Request Feedback"). Several actions contained rules for triggers and instructions that ran a standard form of conversation around the projects.

Syntax and Structure: The syntax featured keywords such as "assign", "update", and "request" — followed by placeholders for task info, project updates, or feedback specifics. The data were structured this way so that the model would know how to treat user prompts as actions that completed the predefined steps of the project collaboration process.

User Interaction: Project team members could trigger actions with short, clear, and natural-language prompts such as "Assign a task for the next sprint" or "Request feedback on the latest code update." Team members could step in and out of the conversation without the need for extensive instructions, leveraging the Menu Actions Pattern for dynamic interactions, regardless of their expertise.

Smart Prompt Handling: It featured intelligent features that allowed it to understand user intent, adapt to prompt variations, and accommodate diverse users, all of which contributed to a more seamless, user-centred experience.

Results

Efficient Project Management: Team members could easily assign tasks, update progress, and request feedback as needed, helping keep everyone on the same page and facilitating productive collaboration.

Consistency Across Teams: The standardized menus loaded from the two libraries ensured that the same response types related to a project could be used across teams.

Adaptive to Varied Input: With different user prompts, the model reduced the errors that limiters could introduce into the overall user experience and the experience of users with different communication tools.

Knowledge Sharing: One of the knowledge-sharing tools that was used by a project team was The Menu Actions Pattern. Best practices were established for common project collaboration actions.

Conclusion

This successfully demonstrated the transformative impact of the Menu Actions Pattern on team interactions at the tech company, as it used it to improve project collaboration. This enabled the organisation to efficiently, effectively, and consistently manage its collaborative software development projects. A Note on Menu Actions Pattern — Case Study

SEMANTIC FILTER PATTERN

Large language models excel at understanding and manipulating text like no other. Despite its amazing capabilities, the Semantic Filter Pattern is a very powerful one that allows you to pull out or adapt information based on very well-defined semantic rules. This pattern goes beyond the surface and considers meaning, not just at the syntactic level as common filters do. This pattern is particularly useful in situations where we want to ensure that the returned results maintain rich contextual relationships and semantic meaning, thereby acting as a micro-adjustment control that allows developers to fine-tune the results from our models according to the desired specifications [11]. In this section, we will examine the defining features of the Semantic Filter Pattern, including its adjustable parameters and capabilities, as well as its various domains of use, in order to better understand its role in improving the relevance and accuracy of text generation [12].

Example 1: GDPR Email Data Redaction

Scenario: A company based in the EU must comply with GDPR rules when sharing information **via** email. To comply with GDPR, the company must secure data like names, addresses, or contact details that are sensitive personal information.

Semantic Filter Instructions: This also applies to any explicit personal information, such as names, addresses, contact info, etc., and to preserving the entirety of the email as such.

Application

To automatically redact sensitive personal information from outgoing emails, the Semantic Filter Pattern is implemented. It does so by removing explicit mentions of personal data, ensuring it goes hand in hand with GDPR and thus preserving the semantic context.

Example 2: Text Transformation For Content Moderation

Scenario: Advanced Content Moderation for User Posts on Social Media Platform. The well-being of the online media environment is what the Platform is all about.

Semantic Filter Instructions: Recognize trends in explicit language, offensive terms, and inappropriate content, while retaining the overall context and meaning of user posts.

Application: This is the Semantic Filter Pattern, which allows for moderation and modification of user-generated content. This improves content moderation as it ensures that the posts made by users are free from language that violates the rules of decency on the platform through its semantic understanding, as it detects and removes profane words.

The following examples from the real world highlight the different ways in which the Semantic Filter Pattern can be implemented for practical use cases where certain semantic criteria need to be addressed (i.e., content must be filtered for privacy compliance in communication or filtering within online communities in order to maintain a positive experience, etc.).

Case Study: Improving Privacy Compliance in Healthcare Communications

Background

Scenario: A healthcare organization that values patient privacy and follows strict healthcare regulations was looking for a secure way to share medical reports and updates. To address this, the Semantic Filter Pattern was used to avoid sharing sensitive information at the patient level while maintaining the necessary context from the communication in question.

Objective

The main goal was to ensure privacy compliance by adding a semantic filter that would allow the organization to automatically identify and redact explicit patient details like names, addresses, and MI numbers in medical reports and communications shared within the organization.

Implementation: Semantic Criteria Definition

Developers established semantic filters that specified sensitive patient information that required redaction, including names, addresses, and medical identification numbers.

Integration into Communication Systems

The Semantic Filter Pattern was also embedded into the organization's communication pipeline, and every outgoing medical report and update was filtered through the privacy enhancer.

Maintain the medical context

Because we want to keep the reports in a medical context, we paid special attention to keep the reports from going out of context. The model was trained to redact sensitive patient information while preserving important medical terms, such as diagnoses and treatment information.

Results

Privacy Compliance: The Semantic Filter Pattern. The semantic filter pattern successfully recognized and redacted explicit patient details from the dataset, complying with healthcare privacy regulations and data protection standards.

Preservation of Medical Relevance: Keeping the medical context intact in the reports allowed the organization to ensure that the information stayed relevant and valuable among healthcare professionals.

Efficiency in Communication: As a result, the semantic filter facilitated smoother communication workflows, enabling staff to share medical updates by default without manually redacting sensitive information, saving time and minimizing the risk of human error.

Conclusion

In particular, the introduction of the Semantic Filter Pattern emerged as a critical factor in upholding privacy compliance within the healthcare organization. This approach struck a balance between protecting sensitive patient information and preserving the vital medical context, enabling it to effectively redact personally identifiable information whilst also providing a fundamentally efficient means of communication. In this case study, we have seen how the Semantic Filter Pattern can be effectively used and how we can adapt it to industry requirements where privacy and compliance are of utmost importance.

CONCLUSION

The revolutionary potential of prompt patterns in improving the effectiveness and interactivity of large language models (LLMs) is highlighted in the chapter's conclusion. Users can customize their AI interactions to deliver more accurate, captivating, and contextually relevant results by leveraging techniques such as gaming patterns, meta-language production, recipe structures, and semantic filtering. These techniques foster dynamic, user-focused experiences by advancing communication, learning processes, and decision-making capabilities. Moreover, the chapter highlights the necessity of ongoing innovation in prompt design to accommodate the shifting demands across various sectors. From educational tools and professional communication to healthcare applications, these patterns have the capacity to revolutionize how humans engage with AI systems—making them more intuitive, effective, and responsive. As AI technologies continue to evolve, the development and implementation of such prompt patterns will remain critical in maximizing their potential, driving technological progress, and enhancing user interaction.

REFERENCES

[1] L. Wang, R. Song, W. Guo, and H. Yang, "Exploring prompt pattern for generative artificial intelligence in automatic question generation", *Interact. Learn. Environ.,* vol. 33, no. 3, pp. 2559-2584, 2024.
[http://dx.doi.org/10.1080/10494820.2024.2412082]

[2] J. White, S. Hays, Q. Fu, J. Spencer-Smith, and D.C. Schmidt, "ChatGPT Prompt Patterns for Improving Code Quality, Refactoring, Requirements Elicitation, and Software Design", Mar. 11, 2023.
[http://dx.doi.org/10.48550/arXiv.2303.07839]

[3] C. Fabricatore, and X. López, "Using gameplay patterns to gamify learning experiences," in *Proceedings of the 8th European Conference on Game Based Learning*, C. Busch, Ed. Academic Conferences and Publishing International Limited, 2014, pp. 110–117.
[http://dx.doi.org/10.13140/2.1.2275.5844]

[4] J. Kang, M. Liu, and W. Qu, "Using gameplay data to examine learning behavior patterns in a serious game", *Comput. Human Behav.,* vol. 72, pp. 757-770, 2017.
[http://dx.doi.org/10.1016/j.chb.2016.09.062]

[5] N. Caporusso, T. Helms, and P. Zhang, "A meta-language approach for machine learning," in *Advances in Artificial Intelligence, Software and Systems Engineering*, T. Ahram, Ed., in *Advances in Intelligent Systems and Computing*, vol. 965. Cham, Switzerland: Springer International Publishing, 2020, pp. 192–201.
[http://dx.doi.org/10.1007/978-3-030-20454-9_19]

[6] A. Wolff, and P. Forbrig, "Pattern catalogs using the pattern language meta language," *Electron. Commun. EASST*, vol. 25, 2010.
[http://dx.doi.org/10.14279/TUJ.ECEASST.25.371]

[7] T. Senath, K. Athukorala, R. Costa, S. Ranathunga, and R. Kaur, "Large language models for ingredient substitution in food recipes using supervised fine-tuning and direct preference optimization," Dec. 6, 2024.
[http://dx.doi.org/10.48550/arXiv.2412.04922]

[8] G. Bagler, and N. Singh, "Data-driven investigations of culinary patterns in traditional recipes across the world," in *2018 IEEE 34th International Conference on Data Engineering Workshops (ICDEW)*, Paris, France, 2018, pp. 157–162.
[http://dx.doi.org/10.1109/ICDEW.2018.00033]

[9] M. Desmond, and M. Brachman, "Exploring prompt engineering practices in the enterprise", Mar. 13, 2024.
[http://dx.doi.org/10.48550/arXiv.2403.08950]

[10] J. White, "A prompt pattern catalog to enhance prompt engineering with ChatGPT", Feb. 21, 2023.
[http://dx.doi.org/10.48550/arXiv.2302.11382]

[11] M. Moundas, J. White, and D. C. Schmidt, "Prompt patterns for structured data extraction from unstructured text," *arXiv:2401.04658*, Jan. 2024.

[12] K.J. Villardar, and C. J. Aliac, "Semantic decomposition and selective context filtering: Text processing techniques for context-aware NLP-based systems," in *Intelligent Systems and Applications. IntelliSys 2025*, K. Arai, Ed., Lecture Notes in Networks and Systems, vol. 1554. Cham, Switzerland: Springer, 2025.
[http://dx.doi.org/10.1007/978-3-031-99965-9_15]

CHAPTER 9

The Clue: The Power of Few-Shots

Abstract: Few-shot prompting, a groundbreaking technique in natural language processing (NLP), is explored in this chapter as a way for large language models (LLMs) to master tasks with minimal examples. The chapter delves into the core mechanisms, applications, and implications of the approach, placing specific focus on its utility in sentiment analysis. Unlike traditional task-specific instructions, few-shot prompting enables models to extrapolate from a limited set of input-output examples and make accurate predictions on new, unseen data. This paradigm shift enhances the adaptability of LLMs, allowing them to tackle diverse tasks without the need for extensive training datasets. The chapter showcases how this technique equips LLMs to effectively analyze sentiments, detect emotions, and categorize textual data with impressive precision, even in scenarios where data is sparse. Moreover, it addresses the challenges inherent in this approach, such as issues with the interpretability of model outputs, inherent biases in training data, and the complexities of generalizing performance across varied tasks. Ethical considerations are also discussed, highlighting the need for transparency and fairness in deploying such systems. Through real-world examples and detailed case studies, the chapter illustrates the transformative impact of few-shot prompting on evolving capabilities of LLMs. This method not only enhances the practical utility of these models but also broadens their potential applications across diverse domains, underscoring their role in advancing the field of NLP.

Keywords: Few-shot prompting, Large Language Models (LLMs), Model generalization, Model interpretability, Natural Language Processing (NLP), Sentiment analysis.

INTRODUCTION

Few-shot prompting has been one of the most striking methods to guide large language models for in-time formats and tasks, and this has become a hot topic in the quickly evolving field of natural language processing (NLP). Indeed, this chapter specifically elucidates the mechanisms, applications and implications of few-shot prompting in depth [1]. This paper is focused on sentiment analysis, giving a canonical domain to disentangle the wonders and surprising power that few-shot prompting affords when it comes to steering language models. Few-shot prompting represents a paradigm shift in natural language processing (NLP) by enabling language models to learn and generalize from only a handful of

Sumit Tripathi

examples. This sets it apart and shows its versatility; models learn a new task with very little data. However, few-shot prompting is fundamental because it allows large-scale NLP systems to infer new tasks and data given just a few examples. For instance, in the context of few-shot prompting for sentiment analysis, we could demonstrate an application of few-shot prompting, allowing language models to learn about more subtle or complex emotions and opinions contained in the textual data. Studying its mechanics in this particular setting enables readers to appreciate the transformations that may occur when a variety of NLP tasks are prompted with few-shot data [2].

This chapter explains in detail the innovative methods of few-shot prompting and provides an idealistic perspective on them in natural language processing. So what our readers find out as they go through this exploration is how few-shot prompting plays its role in the progress of language models and ultimately what its effect is on the progress of NLP capabilities as such.

Understanding Few-Shot Prompting

Introducing few-shot prompting brings a drastic change in the instructions provided to the language model, compared to traditional approaches, where you provide clear and task-oriented instructions for how to operate. Instead, it uses example-rich context, or input/output pairs, to provide the language model with everything it needs to learn [3]. This subtle shift from being told exactly what to do to being able to discern operations melds into the model's efficiency in deriving contextual correlation rather than being constrained to rigid instructions, thus allowing it to become a more malleable entity capable of performing a wide array of tasks with or without preset programming. In the realm of large language models like GPT-3. 5, which are trained to anticipate the next word in a sequence based on the preceding context, few-shot prompting leverages the model's inherent predictive ability. Users elegantly guide the model to learn and generalize the patterns through examples, which enables the model to apply the knowledge in new, unseen contexts [4]. Humanized version: Acknowledging that few-shot prompting is a highly dynamic process in which language models learn and adapt from the examples provided rather than relying on rigid, rules-based programming [5].

Few-shot prompting is somewhat like a guided learning process wherein users supply examples for the model to understand general patterns and associations [6]. By providing the model with examples that clarify the desired output for specific inputs, we enable a more refined and contextually sensitive response approach. What makes a few-shot prompting powerful is the ability to leverage the input-output examples and use them to instruct the model to do what we want,

an example of a prompt, which can represent to us the last resource in tapping the true potential of large language models. Figure 1 shows the whole process of few-shot learning.

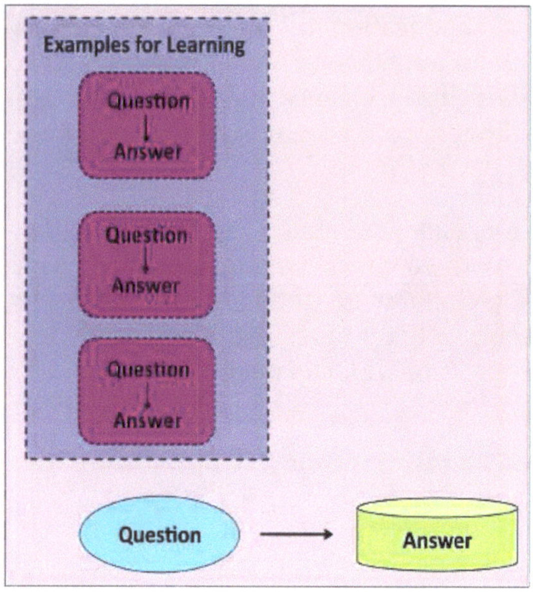

Fig. (1). Few Shot Learning.

A Specific Use Case: Few-Shot Prompting in the Sentiment Analysis Problem

Task Description:

Say, for instance, you wanted to train a language model for sentiment analysis, which is when you judge the sentiment of short text passages. While conventional methods could give explicit rules for sentiment classification, few-shot prompting gives examples for the model to follow.

Few-Shot Prompting Example:

Example Input:

"I just read the best book, and I'm so excited!

Output/Sentiment Label:

Positive

Example Input:

"I'm very upset by the customer service experience; it was terrible.

Output/Sentiment Label:

Negative

Example Input:

"I went to the event, and it was alright, nothing special."

Label: ↑-- Sentiment of the Text Data (↑-- includes the output as fine-tuning data)

Neutral

Guiding the Model:

You use few-shot prompting to give the language model a few example sentences labelled with the correct classes so the model can learn what constitutes positive, negative, or neutral sentiment. The model does not learn rigid rules for sentiment classification; it learns to determine sentiment by picking up on contextual clues in the examples.

Application:

Now, with this few-shot training data, when a user gives the model a new text passage, it can use what it learned to predict the sentiment, positive, negative or neutral, associated with it. This illustrates that few-shot prompting enables the model to extrapolate and apply learned information to make predictions, including in real-world situations, without needing extensive amount of task-specific coding.

Flexibility in Modelling Constraints: The Edges of Self-Inflicted Limitations

In few-shot prompting, a subtle conflict arises between explicit flexibility and self-imposed constraints, further enriching the complexity of language model behavior.

Self-imposed boundaries create a midpoint between flexible yet unfocused language models and constrained yet well-behaved hard-coded ones. It illustrates the model's ability to respond within constrained environments, enabling users to set its behaviour without writing concrete rules. This careful balancing act provides the basis for the success of few-shot prompting; it gives the user a mechanism for aligning the model outputs to a degree of specificity, without necessitating a similar level of specificity in the prompting mechanism.

Vast Dimensions of Few-Shot Prompting

Notably, few-shot prompting not only enables language models to be adaptive but also leads to their versatility over various tasks. In this example, we demonstrate the flexibility of this method, while avoiding an explicit mention of the sentiment analysis task: “I really hated this coffee, it was roasted too much and tasted burned.” Utilizing the patterns learned from earlier examples, the model automatically adds “Negative” for the sentiment output.

Example: Extending the Task

Here, we see the model's ability to generalize and transfer learned concepts to a new task. In the absence of explicit instructions for sentiment analysis, the model generalizes its knowledge and successfully identifies the input as having a negative sentiment. This demonstrates the amazing power of few-shot prompting to allow language models to automatically generalise well outside the space of the training tasks.

Variants of the pattern for improvement: Adaptation and refinement

Few-shot prompting is also great at optimizing patterns for better learning by iteratively adjusting to relevant context, threads, and similar patterns. The model becomes increasingly adept at performing diverse tasks as it builds on its understanding of patterns provided by user examples. This continuous learning process enhances accuracy as well as increases the adaptability of the model to respond well to a diverse range of inputs. Few-shot prompting then acts like an interactive pitfall, guiding a language model through a form of a learned progress cycle [7]. This enables the model to repeatedly refine its performance on each task while still maintaining generality, which is ideal for users seeking a robust, adaptable solution. It finds its way around preset boundaries, growing broader and broader, leaving the user with a still-valid tool for the ever more complex jobs at hand.

Fine-Tuning from More Examples

As the model refines over time, the first batch of examples is just a starting point. Few-shot prompting truly shines during iterative refinement, whereby the model's learning can be accelerated *via* more exposure to entries. Let's consider an example:

For example, lie: Its Dataset Extending

Assume the first examples for sentiment analysis are simple examples. Through adding more complex examples, like those with nuanced opinions or indirect statements, the model hones its ability to recognize, interpret, and manage the subtleties found in closer statements.

Few-shot prompting: Issues and challenges

Few-shot prompting has great potential but brings complexity that must be carefully considered. Well, a very significant challenge is interpretability, and a particular instance highlights this subtle challenge.

Example: Difficult to Interpret

When the model returns a sentiment label in a black-box manner, it can be challenging to understand how it came up with such labels. It is important to note that the model itself might assign a sentiment without giving the user any visibility as to what specific words or phrases in the text it used to make its decision. This lack of transparency can lead to challenges of interpretability when interpreting the outputs of the model. Especially in important applications like sentiment analysis, researchers and developers must know how language models make their decisions. This model interpretability challenge leads to further examination of techniques that can be used to understand the inner workings of the model. Through this exploration, we aim to increase the level of transparency so that users and stakeholders can see and understand the decision-making process.

To better understand the contributions of different input components to the output, techniques like attention mechanisms, layer-wise relevance propagation, or saliency maps are being studied. Working to solve interpretability challenges thus aims to create trust that the model's decisions can be understood and analysed by users to understand and hold accountable how the model generates its outputs. The quest for interpretability is, in fact, part of the bigger picture towards responsible and ethical deployment of AI, helping us understand better how these models make decisions.

Few-Shot Prompting: Ethical Implications and Responsible Use

It is important to navigate the ethical landscape of few-shot prompting, which requires careful consideration; thus, a conscientious and responsible approach is necessary. A particular case highlights one of the key ethical issues.

Example: Mitigating Biases

This highlights the importance of effective mitigation efforts, given how extremely potentially problematic model predictions can be. This issue is acknowledged by developers who implement approaches designed to identify and mitigate biases at the few-shot prompting stage. These steps are to encourage responsible AI development.

Imagine a scenario in which you train a language model using examples of sentiment analysis that contain biased language by accident. If not addressed, the model may learn and continue to perpetuate such biases, possibly resulting in outputs that are unfair or discriminatory. In response to this, developers use bias detection systems to detect possible biases in the training data.

This is when mitigation techniques are introduced, where the model is altered or tuned to decrease the effect of biases. With this approach, the output of the model is then refined further to ensure that the model output is aligned with ethical standards and produces fair and inclusive output. Developers are trying to make their language models not only performant but also fair by reducing biases, a major concern in algorithmic fairness and the equitable treatment of users from diverse groups. This is an example of how developers can take proactive measures to address bias and shows how responsible AI development matters while using language models in practice.

A Look Ahead to the Evolving Landscape of Few-Shot Prompting

Few-shot prompting can change the NLP landscape. This anticipated modality with multimodal inputs is an exciting development, opening up avenues and possibilities previously out of reach within the confines of text.

In this post, I am going to cover some examples.

So, in future few-shot prompting versions, they may allow a seamless integration of these multimodal inputs, and the language models will not only understand text but also images and other modalities. This ground-breaking leap into multimodal capacities paves the way for richer, more integrated applications of language processing in various domains. For example, a user might input a combination of text and an image, prompting the model to generate outputs that consider both modalities. This could improve the contextuality and depth of language models, enabling more nuanced and diverse applications in areas such as content creation, image captioning, and beyond. As a paradigm for adapting general capabilities to specific tasks, few-shot prompting seems to be an agile mechanism that signals language models' leap into an era where they can naturally receive a wide variety of input modalities and provide the appropriate output modality. This evolution marks a paradigm shift, operating beyond the realm of traditional text-based interactions and setting new frontiers for what language models can achieve.

Across the sprawling landscape of natural language processing methods, few-shot prompting is an exemplar of ingenuity: flexible, responsive, and potent. This approach underlines a profound adaptation of language models, not just to excel at age-old tasks such as sentiment prediction, but also to prepare them for emerging ones.

Example: Generate Conversation

We demonstrate how few-shot prompting can enable language models to learn dialogue generation beyond simply performing sentiment analysis. Users can provide examples of conversational patterns they would like to see in the generated sentences, and the model, in turn, learns to generate them as dynamic, contextually relevant dialogues. This transformative ability closely resembles human interaction, and as a result, language models become interactive conversational agents rather than mere information retrieval tools.

With the combination of multimodal integration and conversation generation, this work highlights the exciting opportunities afforded by few-shot prompting to push the frontiers of language models further." Not only does it mark a technological milestone, but it also opens new realms for future interaction in which computers can act with human-like understanding and expression. But few-shot prompting, it seems, could still hold many more secrets as we learn more about its capabilities and its relation to the algorithms of natural language processing.

FEW-SHOT LEARNING: A CASE STUDY IN IMAGE CLASSIFICATION

Introduction:

Few-shot learning is a machine learning setting where only a small amount of labelled data is provided for learning the sample distribution. One of the applications of few-shot learning can be seen in image classification. We use this case study to demonstrate how this approach resolves challenges related to data scarcity.

Problem Statement:

Let's visualize a situation where a company wants to deploy an image classification system for a particular category of products in its inventory. Because of limited time and available resources, the labelled dataset for training is small.

Traditional Approach:

In this case, for a standard image classification task, we would need a relatively big labeled data set to be able to properly train a deep neural network. This could mean gathering and labelling tens of thousands or millions of images for each category of products.

Few-Shot Learning Solution:

Challenging the "Big is Beautiful" paradigm, the company embraces few-shot learning and is significantly more efficient and resource-aware. And instead of needing huge quantities of labelled training data — the sorts of things those sorts of systems tend to rely on — this system learns from a few, perhaps several, examples of the entire product class.

Implementation Steps:

• **Model Architecture:**

The backbone is a pre-trained convolutional neural network (CNN), including the few-shot learning module, enabling the integration of new classes with few examples into the model.

• **Dataset Preparation:**

This (meta) "training" is conducted on the basis of being provided with very few, labelled examples for each category of product (1-5 images). This small set of examples is intended for the model to generalize from.

• **Few-Shot Learning Module:**

This few-shot learning module can contain methods based on meta-learning or episodic training. When training, the model is presented with episodes where it teaches itself to adapt rapidly to novel classes with few examples.

Results:

Despite the limited number of labelled data, the few-shot learning approach yields remarkable performance. The model shows the ability to precisely classify unseen products despite being given only a small number of examples during adaptation.

Advantages:

• **Resource Efficiency:**

It demands orders of magnitude less labelled data than traditional methods, thus it is cheaper.

- **Adaptability:**

The model demonstrated that it can learn to adapt to new classes, enabling the system to scale and be retrained for changes within 1% of the product inventory.

- **Quick Deployment:**

It is easy to set up, adaptable, and responsive to changes in environments.

Challenges:

Overfitting the small number of examples carries a risk of overfitting, so regularization techniques have to be applied carefully.

- **Class Imbalance:**

With an uneven number of examples per class, predictions may be biased.

Conclusion:

Few-shot learning serves as a real useful technology that can save much time when used correctly. This enables the company to perform accurate image classification, showing the benefits of few-shot methods on a practical task.

CASE STUDY: FEW-SHOT LEARNING FOR PERSONALIZED RECOMMENDATION IN E-COMMERCE

Introduction:

In the e-commerce domain, few-shot learning, a strong paradigm for generalization in supervised learning, is innovatively applied for personalized recommendation systems.

Problem Statement:

A major e-commerce company wants to enhance its recommendation engine to drive greater user engagement and conversions. But collecting a considerable labelled data set concerning each individuals' preferences is infeasible, given the privacy issues involved and the requirement for the recommendations to be timely and accurate.

Traditional Approach:

Conventional recommendation systems typically employ collaborative filtering or content-based approaches, which necessitate having a lot of historical data for every user. Constructing a complete user-item interaction matrix requires substantial resources and might not reflect changing user tastes effectively.

Few-Shot Learning Solution:

Identify the problem: The e-commerce platform recognizes that common methods for collecting and processing user interactions are too cumbersome for its target demographic.

Implementation Steps:

- **User Representation**

User behaviour is encoded using a pre-trained neural network that only considers the history of limited past interactions.

- **Few-Shot Learning Module:**

The recommendation system integrates a few-shot learning module.

Few-Shot Learning in Recommender Systems: During training, the model is provided with few-shot episodes to mimic situations wherein it must make recommendations to a user based on a small set of interactions made by that user.

- **Adapt to User preferences:**

It learns patterns from these and adjusts swiftly to changing user preferences of new users with minimal data. Meta-learning techniques enable the system to generalize and provide accurate recommendations even in scenarios where the user history is limited.

Results:

Through this few-shot learning approach, the accuracy of personalized recommendations is greatly enhanced even for users with a sparse interaction history. As users explore more of a platform, they are provided with appropriate recommendations that align with their changing tastes, which results in improved click-through and conversion rates.

Advantages

- **Limited Data Personalization:**

By utilizing few-shot learning, the model can act on users with no — or little interaction data, leading to personalized recommendations.

- **Quick Adaptation:**

It quickly learns and adapts to the incoming changes to user preferences and delivers relevant recommendations even with almost no user history.

- **Enhanced User Engagement:**

By using personalized recommendations, users are more likely to find what they want and buy what they like.

Challenges

- **Cold-Start Users:**

Users with very little interaction history are difficult to handle by the system, and they may need some cold-start origin strategies.

- **User Representations Quality:**

User representations play an important role and must always be fine-tuned for the model to work effectively.

Custom recommendation systems have been significantly altered by few-shot learning, particularly in e-commerce. Recommendation engines often require a lot of user interaction data and a huge dataset to provide individualized recommendations. However, few-shot learning makes it possible for these algorithms to produce incredibly relevant recommendations even in the case of low user data [8]. Few-shot learning models work well in scenarios where companies just know what consumers have previously interacted with—clicks, views, or purchases, for instance—because they can accurately anticipate outcomes from a limited number of samples. This is particularly helpful when there is a lack of user data, such as when a consumer is brand-new or hasn't used the platform often. The model may generate pertinent recommendations for the user even if it only learns from a small number of data points. In such contexts, few-shot learning shows promise in upending the conventional recommendation engine. A few-shot learning approach allows business operations to provide highly targeted recommendations even in situations when data is limited, instead of relying on vast amounts of data. It might completely change the way recommendation systems operate, giving consumers a better experience in terms of increased engagement and conversions while using less data to operate efficiently.

CONCLUSION

The importance of few-shot prompting for the development of natural language processing (NLP) is emphasized at the end of the chapter. Because it allows large language models (LLMs) to learn efficiently from a small number of examples, this technique has completely changed the way AI systems approach new jobs. Few-shot prompting is notably resource-efficient, empowering models to perform complex tasks—such as sentiment analysis—without necessitating extensive amounts of labelled data. However, the discussion also highlights several challenges inherent to this approach, including issues with model interpretability and the risk of inherent biases in training data. Despite these obstacles, few-shot prompting remains a cornerstone technique for enhancing the adaptability and efficiency of AI systems across diverse applications. Its ability to generalize from minimal input establishes it as a critical tool in reducing data dependency while broadening the scope of task-oriented AI capabilities. As the field of AI evolves, few-shot prompting is projected to assume an even greater role in shaping more versatile and data-efficient language models. The chapter advocates for sustained research efforts to mitigate the risks of bias, improve interpretability, and address ethical concerns, ensuring the responsible and impactful implementation of this transformative approach.

REFERENCES

[1] Y. Zhang, Y. Xu, and F. Dong, "An enhanced few-shot text classification approach by integrating topic modeling and prompt-tuning", *Neurocomputing,* vol. 617, p. 129082, 2025. [http://dx.doi.org/10.1016/j.neucom.2024.129082]

[2] T. Schick, and H. Schütze, "True few-shot learning with prompts—a real-world perspective", *Trans. Assoc. Comput. Linguist.,* vol. 10, pp. 716-731, 2022. [http://dx.doi.org/10.1162/tacl_a_00485]

[3] T.B. Brown, "Language models are few-shot learners", Jul. 22, 2020. [http://dx.doi.org/10.48550/arXiv.2005.14165]

[4] L. Wang, R. Chen, and L. Li, "Knowledge-guided prompt learning for few-shot text classification", *Electronics (Basel),* vol. 12, no. 6, p. 1486, 2023. [http://dx.doi.org/10.3390/electronics12061486]

[5] W. Chen, C. Si, Z. Zhang, L. Wang, Z. Wang, and T. Tan, "Semantic prompt for few-shot image recognition", Mar. 24, 2023. [http://dx.doi.org/10.48550/arXiv.2303.14123]

[6] Y. Gu, X. Han, Z. Liu, and M. Huang, "PPT: Pre-trained prompt tuning for few-shot learning," in *Proceedings of the 60th Annual Meeting of the Association for Computational Linguistics (Volume 1: Long Papers)*, Dublin, Ireland, 2022, pp. 8416–8433. [http://dx.doi.org/10.18653/v1/2022.acl-long.576]

[7] M. Mosbach, T. Pimentel, S. Ravfogel, D. Klakow, and Y. Elazar, Few-shot fine-tuning *vs.* in-context learning: A fair comparison and evaluation., May 30, 2023. [http://dx.doi.org/10.18653/v1/2023.findings-acl.779]

[8] G. Izacard, "Atlas: Few-shot learning with retrieval augmented language models", Nov. 16, 2022. [http://dx.doi.org/10.48550/arXiv.2208.03299]

CHAPTER 10

Harnessing the Power of Azure GPT Playground for Advanced Prompt Engineering

Abstract: The Azure GPT Playground's vast potential is explored in this chapter, with an emphasis on how it may be used for sophisticated prompt engineering in AI-driven applications. It begins by guiding readers through the step-by-step process of establishing an Azure account and navigating the GPT Playground *via* the Azure portal. Readers are introduced to strategies for crafting effective prompts that harness the full capability of GPT models, supported by a thorough explanation of the Azure OpenAI Service, the foundational platform for the Playground. The chapter provides meticulous guidelines for setting up the GPT service to ensure optimal performance. It covers essential practices for monitoring usage and managing resources, equipping users with the tools to maintain efficiency and scalability. Extensive attention is given to the GPT Playground's customizable parameters, such as temperature and maximum tokens, which allow users to fine-tune output for specific needs—whether in content creation, customer interaction, or the development of educational resources. Additionally, the chapter explores integration possibilities with other Azure services, notably Logic Apps, demonstrating how such linkages can enhance operational workflows. It outlines practical strategies for tracking expenses and managing costs associated with GPT model use, ensuring financial oversight. Ethical considerations are highlighted throughout, with a strong emphasis on data privacy, security measures, and regulatory compliance, ensuring readers are equipped to utilize these AI-powered tools responsibly. This structured approach provides a well-rounded framework for leveraging the Azure GPT Playground effectively and ethically.

Keywords: Azure GPT playground, Azure OpenAI service, Customizable parameters, Ethical AI use, Generative Pre-trained Transformers (GPT), Prompt engineering.

INTRODUCTION

AI is transforming industries with applications ranging from content writing and video generation to customer support and data analytics. The AI revolution is driven by the development of Generative Pre-trained Transformers (GPT), especially the GPT models from OpenAI, which have set new standards in natural language processing (NLP) [1]. They can engage in multispecies, in which they have the ability to replicate the physical experience almost human because they

Sumit Tripathi

are able to access both worlds. Experimental power with powerful models — *via* Azure GPT Playground. It is an all-purpose tool for many types of users, including developers, data scientists, educators, and business people. The GPT Playground allows users to create content, automate tedious tasks, and experiment with new ideas in AI-powered creativity. This chapter will prepare readers for the Azure portal, the GPT Playground, how to generate effective prompts, and how to use all that within larger workflows [2].

SETTING UP THE AZURE PORTAL

Before we proceed, let us separate Azure login using Terraform from the use of GPT Playground. In this lesson, you walk through the process of creating an Azure account, setting up the necessary resources, and getting familiar with the Azure portal's UI, preparing you for a proper start with Azure's powerful tools.

Azure Account: Creation and Configuration

Creating an Azure account is the first step for creating access to all of the services Microsoft Azure offers, including the GPT Playground.

Visit the Azure Portal

Open a browser and go to https://portal.azure.com. Similar to a "welcome mat," the Azure portal is the main entrance to cloud services offered by Microsoft Azure.

Sign Up for a Free Account

Select the blue "Start free" link to begin the sign-up process. Microsoft Azure offers a free tier, along with $200 in credits for your first 30 days. Without any upfront cost, this free offering allows you to try out Azure services, including accessing the OpenAI GPT models.

Provide Personal Information

To sign up, you must provide your name, email address, and other personal information, including payment information. Note that a credit card is needed for verification, but charges will only apply if usage goes above the free tier limits.

Identity Verification

A phone call or a small refundable charge to the credit card may be the identity verification step. This is a way to confirm the Azure account is valid and trusted.

Finalize Registration

As soon as the verification process is completed, the Azure account is unlocked for all services in the Azure portal.

Navigating the Azure Portal

The Azure portal is the single place to create and manage all your cloud services and resources. This interface is critical for being able to navigate Azure's tools, including the GPT Playground.

- **Dashboard Overview:** The Azure portal dashboard is a central command center for managing Azure resources. A highly customizable build, allowing users to pin frequently accessed services and resources for convenient connections. These customizations help users optimize active projects and track resource usage.
- **Resource Groups:** In Azure, all the resources are grouped in defined groups called "Resource Groups". These groups - they are containers that have resources that belong together for a solution or project. As an example, the "AI_Projects" resource group can be created , which helps to organize all GPT-related services together for ease of management and deploy these resources.
- **Process to Create & Manage Resource Groups:**

Creating a Resource Group

i. Select the "Resource Groups" section in the Azure Portal. You can access this section from the main menu as well as from the search bar.
ii. Click on "Add" to add a new resource group. Next, users are prompted to name the resource group, then select a geographic region (for example, "East US") that is geographically near the primary user base. Choose a nearby region — This helps to minimize latency and improve the performance of the services in the group.

Resource Management Within Groups

After creating a resource group, you can add resources like the Azure OpenAI Service, storage accounts, or databases to it. By nesting the files within a structured directory hierarchy, you create an intuitive relationship between the resources that are central to an AI project, facilitating their deployment and maintenance.

Create Azure Open AI Service

We host the GPT models through the Azure OpenAI Service , which is paramount to the GPT Playground. This service is easy to set up and is crucial for using GPT capabilities.

In the search bar, type the Azure OpenAI Service:

Step 1: Navigate to the Azure Portal. Search for Azure OpenAI Service 1. All of the GPT models that power the Playground are available through this service.

Step 2: Create a New OpenAI Resource:

i. To establish the service, click on "Create. Users will be asked to choose the resource group, region, and instance details.
ii. Select the resource group from step 2 (for example, "AI_Projects") and pick a region closest to primary users to reduce latency.
iii. Name your OpenAI resource something unique and descriptive to avoid confusion with other resources (*i.e.*, "GPT-Playground-Instance").

Configure the Service

Choose the right Pricing tier depending on expected usage. Free tier — limited access. Best for early testing and experimentation. For extensive usage, consider upgrading to a paid tier user plan, which provides significantly greater token quantity with faster processing time.

Review and Deploy

Check the settings to make sure everything is correct after configuring them. Hit "Create" to deploy the service. Deploying this could take a couple of minutes as it sets up the infrastructure needed to run this code in Azure.

Monitoring Deployment

Notify me once the deployment is finished. Once created, you can navigate to the service from the resource group or directly from the dashboard.

Understanding Pricing and Quotas

Azure's OpenAI Service works on a pay-as-you-go basis, where the pricing is based on the number of tokens processed by the GPT models. It is essential to understand the pricing and manage quotas well to prevent getting billed for unwanted usage.

Token Consumption: In GPT Models, a “token” can be as little as a single character or as long as a single word. The fee is determined by the number of tokens executed for every interaction with the model. Keeping track of how many tokens are being used is crucial for cost management, particularly when consuming the service at scale.

Manage quota: Users can configure alerts in Azure that let them know if their usage is getting close to limits set by the administrator. Alerting on egress not only prevents overage in budgets, but also prevents shocking bills if a user consumes above normal levels of egress to a service.

Step 3: Go to the GPT Playground

Now that the Azure OpenAI Service is configured, GPT Playground will be available. In this part, you will get to learn how to navigate the Playground, familiarize yourself with its interface, and tweak settings to make your experience with the GPT models as efficient as possible.

LAUNCHING THE GPT PLAYGROUND: NAVIGATE TO THE PLAYGROUND

GPT Playground is available as an OpenAI service resource in the Azure portal. In the overview section, there’s a link to the “Playground,” which opens a new browser tab.

Exploring the Interface

Prompt Input Area: where the prompts are entered. The model is fundamentally a text input and output machine, and most of the engagement occurs here.

Output Area: This is the area where the AI-generated response will be displayed after submitting your prompt. Users can adjust and improve their prompts based on these answers.

Choose a Model: Through Playground, we can select various versions of the GPT model (*e.g.*, GPT-3, GPT-3. 5). The versions differ in capabilities, and each user needs to select the best version based on their own needs.

Tunable Settings: The Playground provides a number of parameters that can be tuned to impact how the model responds (for example, temperature, maximum tokens, and frequency and presence penalties.

Explaining Adjustable Parameters in Detail

Temperature: This parameter controls how random the model's output is. Higher temperature (*e.g.*, 0.8) makes the model take more creative risks, resulting in diverse and interesting outputs. On the other hand, when the temperature is low (for instance, 0.2), the model becomes more deterministic, generating more predictable and less diverse outputs.

For instance, if the model is set to have a temperature of 0.2 and the user asks it to describe a certain city, it may give a generic answer like, "the city has tall buildings and advanced public transport". With a temperature of 0.8, the model might produce a more creative output: "The city is a sprawling metropolis of glass and steel, with floating gardens and autonomous vehicles zipping through transparent tubes."

Max Tokens: This setting determines how long the responses output by the model will be. Longer token limits yield more comprehensive answers, while shorter limits make answers more concise.

For instance, when asking "Explain the process of photosynthesis," if the max tokens are set to just 50, you may get a response such as: "Photosynthesis is a process where plants use sunlight to synthesize food from carbon dioxide and water." Raising the max tokens to 150 might yield a more expansive definition: "Photosynthesis is the process used by plants, algae, and some bacteria to convert light energy into chemical energy that can be released to fuel the organisms' activities. "Photosynthesis, which includes carbon dioxide and water, and when the sun shines, turns into glucose and oxygen.

Frequency and Presence Penalties: These parameters are designed to help reduce repetitiveness in the output of the model. The frequency penalty limits the repetition of same tokens, while the presence penalty limits repeating ideas/words.

For example, if the model is asked to enumerate the benefits of drinking water, then a frequency penalty of 0 would lead to outputs like: "Drinking water is good for hydration. So is drinking water." And with a frequency penalty of 1, the output could be more varied: "Drinking water can help you stay hydrated, improve skin health, aid digestion, and regulate body temperature."

ITERATIVE PROMPT REFINEMENT

Building good, effective prompts can be an iterative process. It starts with a general prompt, and over a number of iterations with response bites, the prompt is fine-tuned according to the responses received.

Steps for Refining Prompts

- Start Broad — Ask general questions, or make general statements about what you want to learn. The first prompt is supposed to give an idea of what the model assumes.
- Analyze the Output — Read through the response to find qualitative areas where the output might need to be more narrow, specific, or to clarify the NLP model's interpretation.
- Prompt Refinement: Change the prompt text if necessary to contextually widen it, request a specific outcome, or focus on a narrower aspect of the topic. The method of distillation is necessary to train the model to create the most accurate response.

Example of Prompt Refinement

Original Prompt: *"Explain the Internet of Things (IoT) to me."*

Initial Response: The Internet of Things (IoT) refers to a system of interrelated physical objects that are embedded with sensors, software, and other technologies for the purpose of connecting and exchanging data with other devices and systems over the Internet.

A more selective prompt: *"How is IoT applied to smart homes?*

Refined Response: "In smart homes, IoT devices such as thermostats, security cameras, and lighting systems are connected to a central network. This system enables homeowners to monitor and control devices remotely through smartphones or by voice, improving energy efficiency and security."

The user directs the model by iteratively refining prompts, leading to more nuanced and actionable results.

So why waste time reading the same information in different wording?

The GPT Playground has wide-ranging applications across many domains, including content generation, customer service, and consumer-facing tools. In this section, you can find various common use cases that showcase just how versatile and powerful the Playground can be!

CONTENT CREATION

One of the most potent applications for the GPT Playground is content creation. From writing product descriptions to creating blog entries and social media content, the Playground can help speed things up and inspire additional creativity.

Illustration: Generating a product description for a smartwatch tailored for fitness lovers.

- **Prompt:** *"Write a product description for a smartwatch intended for fitness enthusiasts."*
- **Sound:** "Introducing ActiveFit Pro, the ultimate smart watch for fitness lovers. The Affordable ActiveFit Pro smart watch is designed to be your perfect fitness companion, featuring advanced health monitoring capabilities such as heart rate tracking, sleep analysis, and a built-in GPS to help you reach your health goals. Its ruggedized, water-resistant body means it can keep pace with your most demanding workouts, while a long-lasting battery means you can rely on it when you need it most, day after day."

The response above is a clean product description that is ready to copy and paste somewhere, which describes the key features and benefits of the smartwatch, showing off the advantage of using the GPT Playground and how it saves you time and effort in writing.

CUSTOMER SUPPORT AUTOMATION

The GPT Playground can be used in many creative ways, and one thing I am using it for is automating customer support interactions. With the model trained to handle common customer inquiries, businesses can alleviate their human agents' workload and provide them with solutions faster [3].

Example: Assisting a customer having trouble resetting their password.

Prompt: *"A customer asking how to reset their password. How would the chatbot respond?"*

Response: "Click on 'Forgot Password' on the login page to reset your password. You will get a link to create a new password *via* email. Then check your spam folder for that email, or contact support at support. — Pay close attention to the error message you received.

This automated response is clear and succinct with a step-by-step guide, which is perfect for customer service situations.

EDUCATIONAL TOOLS

The GPT Playground can also be used by educators and trainers to generate educational content like quiz questions, explanatory texts, or study materials. The model may be used as a tool to engage in writing content that can help improve the learning curve.

For example, you could do this to make a multiple-choice question about World War I.

Example of prompt and response:

Prompt: *"Write a multiple-choice question about the causes of World War I.*

Response: Which of the following was a major cause of World War I? A) Archduke Franz Ferdinand's assassination, B) The signing of the Treaty of Versailles, C) The rise of the United Nations, D) The Great Depression

Correct Answer: A) Assassination of Archduke Franz Ferdinand.

THE EXTRAORDINARY EDUCATION AND HIGH-QUALITY GPT-POWERED OUTPUT FROM THE GPT PLAYGROUND

Data Analysis and Reporting

GPT models can also make it easier to summarize complex data and create reports, making them powerful tools for analysts and data scientists.

Example: Writing a summary of important details from a quarterly financial report.

Question: "Please summarize the major highlights of the quarterly earnings report of XYZ Corp."

Answer: "ABC Corp's Q1 earnings statement from their financial report reveals a 15% increase in revenue from the last quarter due to well-performing sales in the technology sector. Operating expenses were even, leading to a net profit increase of 10%. The report also notes strong expansion of the Asian market, adding to the overall good performance."

The summary gives a clear and concise overview of the financial report, enabling stakeholders to quickly understand the most relevant details.

Telling Stories and Creative Writing

The GPT Playground is also an impressive creative writing tool. It can select a running time in which to create ideas, get past writer's block, or even draft whole narratives.

For Example, Dystopian novel opening paragraph.

Prompt: *"Write the first paragraph of a dystopian novel set in a small town."*

Reply: "The rain-beaten streets of Millfield resounded with the long-distant toll of the only bell, ringing out in the fog. After sundown, no one dared to go outside, except the old folks who were scared the sun would leave them, too, and the shadow of the old clock tower buried their secrets. But tonight, under a sputtering streetlight, a stranger had come to visit, with him the possibility of revealing the town's buried secrets."

This opening paragraph is vivid and atmospheric, and would work well as the first paragraph of a novel.

SPECIAL FEATURES AND INTEGRATIONS

As great as the GPT Playground is on its own, so much more can be achieved by combining it with other Azure services. In this section, we look at some more advanced features and integrations that can be beneficial for projects and improve workflow.

API Integration

The Azure Open AI API allows developers to embed these GPT capabilities seamlessly into their applications. These dynamic responses and text generation can occur in websites, mobile applications, and any medium that accepts AI-powered text in real time.

Ex: Using GPT in a customer service app that automatically generates responses for customer queries.

Here is a sample code for the integration of your API:

import openai

Set your API key

openai. api_key = “your-api-key”

Make a completion request

response = openai. Completion. create(

engine=”text-davinci-003”,

prompt=”Explain the concept of blockchain technology.,

max_tokens=100

(print(response. choices[0]. text. strip())

This produced a response from the API that I could use in an application. This feature can, for example, be integrated into an automated FAQ tool or even a support chatbot.

Integration with Azure Logic Apps

Azure Logic Apps is a cloud service that allows the creation and automation of workflows without writing code. By integrating GPT-generated content with Logic Apps, users can automate complex processes that involve multiple steps and data sources.

- **Example Workflow**: Automating customer service responses using GPT-generated content.
  - **Trigger**: A new customer inquiry is received *via* email.
  - **Action**: The GPT model generates a response using the API.
  - **Result**: The generated response is automatically sent back to the customer *via* email.

This integration can streamline customer service operations, reduce response times, and improve overall customer satisfaction.

Steps to Create a Workflow with Azure Logic Apps:

1. **Create a New Logic App**: In the Azure portal, navigate to “Logic Apps” and click “Create” to set up a new app.

2. **Choose a Trigger**: Select a trigger for the workflow, such as "When an email is received."
3. **Add an Action**: Integrate the GPT API as an action, where the content generated by the model is used to formulate a response.
4. **Set Up Outputs**: Define the output, such as sending an email response back to the customer.
5. **Test and Deploy**: Run the workflow to ensure it functions correctly, then deploy it in a production environment.

This setup allows the automation of content generation, reduces manual intervention, and ensures consistent communication with customers.

Managing and Monitoring Usage

As the use of the GPT Playground and related services increases, it is essential to monitor resource usage, stay within resource limits, and manage costs effectively.

Monitoring Usage

Monitoring usage helps understand how much of the allocated resources (like tokens) are being used and whether adjustments are needed.

Steps to Monitor Usage

1. **Usage Dashboard**: Access the "Usage + Quotas" section in the Azure OpenAI resource to view current usage statistics. This dashboard provides a detailed breakdown of token usage and remaining quotas.
2. **Set Up Alerts**: Set up usage alerts in the Azure portal to notify when usage approaches a certain threshold. This helps avoid unexpected overages and allows action to be taken before hitting limits.

Scaling Resources

As the use of GPT models grows, there may be a need to scale resources to handle increased demand.

Options for Scaling

- **Upgrading the Plan**: If token limits are regularly hit or response times are slow, consider upgrading to a higher pricing tier. This tier will provide access to more tokens and faster processing times.
- **Adding Instances**: For large-scale applications, additional instances of the OpenAI resource may be needed to handle increased load. This is particularly

important for applications that need to handle a high volume of requests simultaneously.

Cost Management

Effective cost management ensures that the use of Azure services remains sustainable over time.

Tips for Managing Costs

- **Set Budgets**: Use Azure Cost Management + Billing to set budgets for the OpenAI service. This allows tracking of spending and ensures that financial limits are not exceeded.
- **Optimize Prompts**: Optimize prompts to minimize token usage. For example, concise and clear prompts can reduce the number of tokens processed, helping to stay within allocated quotas.

Ensuring Security and Compliance

When using AI services, especially those involving sensitive data, security and compliance are paramount. Azure provides several tools and best practices to ensure that the use of the GPT Playground adheres to industry standards and protects data.

Data Privacy Best Practices

Data privacy is crucial when dealing with AI models that process potentially sensitive information. Here are some best practices to follow:

- **Avoid Sensitive Data**: Avoid inputting personally identifiable information (PII) or confidential data into the GPT Playground. Always anonymize data before using it.
- **Use Encryption**: Ensure that all data interactions with Azure services are encrypted. Azure provides robust encryption options for data at rest and in transit, helping to protect against unauthorized access.

Compliance with Industry Standards

Depending on the type of data being handled, compliance with specific regulations and industry standards, such as GDPR or HIPAA, may be required.

Steps to Ensure Compliance

- **GDPR Compliance**: For organizations handling data from EU citizens, ensure that the use of GPT models complies with the General Data Protection Regulation (GDPR). This includes obtaining explicit consent from users before processing their data and ensuring that data is securely stored and transferred.
- **HIPAA Compliance**: For applications involving healthcare data, ensure that usage aligns with the Health Insurance Portability and Accountability Act (HIPAA). This is essential for protecting patient information and ensuring that all data handling practices meet the required standards.

The Azure GPT Playground is a powerful and versatile tool that opens up new possibilities for users across various industries. Whether automating content creation, enhancing customer service, or exploring creative writing, the GPT models available through Azure can significantly improve efficiency and innovation in various projects.

This chapter has provided a comprehensive guide to setting up the Azure portal, accessing and navigating the GPT Playground, crafting effective prompts, and exploring practical applications [4]. Additionally, advanced features such as API integration and Azure Logic Apps, as well as best practices for managing usage, costs, and compliance, have been covered. By mastering the use of the GPT Playground, it is possible to leverage AI to drive significant improvements in workflows and deliver better outcomes for organizations. Continuous monitoring of usage, effective cost management, and adherence to security and compliance standards are crucial for fully harnessing the potential of AI through Azure. As AI continues to evolve, tools like the Azure GPT Playground will become increasingly integral to the way businesses and individuals innovate, communicate, and solve complex problems.

EXPERIMENTING WITH DIFFERENT GPT PARAMETER SETTINGS ON THE AZURE PORTAL

By varying parameters like temperature, max tokens, and top_p, one can experiment with the various GPT settings made in the Azure Portal, adjust the generated text to suit particular needs, and actually adjust the output to meet specific needs like creativity, accuracy, length, and diversity. When tailored to different use cases, including technical documents, reports, or creative writing, these parameters give users control over the content's structure and style. Exploration aids in optimizing GPT models through a variety of configurations, ensuring that the final content is pertinent to the stated goals.

Example: Generating Content with Different Parameter Settings

This example covers how Azure OpenAI Service parameter settings can affect generated content. The objective of this job is to use several GPT model settings to produce an article about the benefits of AI in healthcare. When the maximum token limit, which controls the response length, and the temperature, which determines inventiveness, is changed, the output is examined [5].

1. Generated Content with High Temperature (0.9) and Max Tokens = 200
   - **Temperature**: 0.9 (High creativity, more randomness)
   - **Max Tokens**: 200 (Shorter output)

GPT Generated Output

Artificial Intelligence (AI) is quickly becoming a game-changer in healthcare, enabling a more personalized and precise approach to patient care. AI systems can process enormous amounts of medical data in seconds, identifying patterns that would take human doctors years to detect. For instance, AI algorithms can predict a patient's risk of developing certain conditions, providing doctors with early warnings and more time to intervene.

Moreover, AI is enabling the creation of tailored treatment plans, helping doctors select the best possible options for patients based on their unique genetic makeup. This individualization in healthcare makes treatment not only more effective but also more efficient, reducing costs and hospital stays.

As AI continues to evolve, it will increasingly shape the future of healthcare, potentially providing even more accurate diagnoses and expanding access to quality care for underserved populations. However, the widespread use of AI must be balanced with ethical considerations and strong data privacy protections.

Analysis

The result is succinct, imaginative, and captivating. While providing a comprehensive introduction to AI in healthcare, it maintains an engaging and stimulating tone. The high temperature setting pushes the model to produce more imaginative and varied content.

2. Generated Content with Low Temperature (0.2) and Max Tokens = 300
   - **Temperature**: 0.2 (Low creativity, more structured and predictable output)
   - **Max Tokens**: 300 (Longer output)

GPT Generated Output

Artificial Intelligence (AI) has a profound impact on the healthcare industry, improving both the quality and efficiency of patient care. AI systems are used for tasks ranging from diagnosing diseases to predicting patient outcomes. One of the key benefits of AI in healthcare is its ability to analyse large volumes of medical data, such as patient records and diagnostic images, to detect diseases early. For example, AI-powered tools can identify patterns in medical imaging data that might be overlooked by human clinicians, allowing for earlier interventions and more accurate diagnoses.

In addition to diagnostics, AI is playing a critical role in personalized medicine. By analysing individual patient data, including genetics, lifestyle, and medical history, AI can help healthcare providers develop customized treatment plans that are more likely to be effective for each patient. This approach not only improves treatment outcomes but also reduces unnecessary treatments, saving time and healthcare resources.

Furthermore, AI is being used to automate administrative tasks, such as scheduling appointments and managing patient records, helping healthcare providers focus more on patient care rather than paperwork. This increased efficiency results in reduced operational costs and faster service delivery.

Analysis

The output, which outlines the use of AI in healthcare, is factual and well-structured. For reports or professional content where accuracy and depth are crucial, a low temperature setting that produces a clear, predictable output would be ideal. With an emphasis on providing a thorough understanding of AI's applications, the information is more extensive and in-depth.

3. Generated Content with Very High Temperature (1.0) and Max Tokens = 100
    - **Temperature**: 1.0 (Max creativity, highly random and abstract)
    - **Max Tokens**: 100 (Shorter output)

GPT Generated Output

AI in healthcare is like a surgeon with the power of a thousand minds, seeing what humans can't. It decodes the future of medicine by uncovering hidden patterns and unveiling potential diagnoses that were once mere hypotheses. Personalized treatments, once a dream, are now a reality, with AI offering customized solutions that change lives. The ability to predict health crises before they emerge might just be the miracle we've all been waiting for. But like all powerful tools, AI must be wielded carefully, respecting patient privacy and ethical boundaries.

Analysis

It is abstract and really creative. Because of the extremely high temperature setting, the output has a more poetic tone and employs complex metaphors. Despite being less structured, the substance makes a powerful emotional appeal. Though it could lack the accuracy required for official paperwork, this is perfect for brainstorming sessions or when you need interesting, creative content.

4. Generated Content with Medium Temperature (0.5) and Max Tokens = 500
   - **Temperature**: 0.5 (Balanced creativity, mix of randomness and structure)
   - **Max Tokens**: 500 (Longer output)

GPT Generated Output

Artificial Intelligence (AI) has emerged as a transformative force in the healthcare industry, offering innovative solutions that improve patient care, streamline operations, and reduce costs. One of the most significant advantages of AI is its ability to process and analyze vast amounts of data far more efficiently than a human ever could. This capability has led to breakthroughs in disease detection, where AI systems are able to identify early signs of diseases such as cancer, heart disease, and diabetes by examining medical images, genetic information, and patient history.

AI also plays a key role in the development of personalized medicine. By analyzing data from diverse sources—such as medical records, genetic information, and lifestyle factors—AI systems can help doctors develop highly customized treatment plans for patients. This personalization increases the likelihood of successful treatment outcomes and minimizes the trial-and-error approach often associated with traditional healthcare methods.

Beyond direct patient care, AI is also improving healthcare administration. Tasks such as scheduling, billing, and managing patient records can now be automated with AI-powered systems, saving healthcare providers both time and money. The efficiency gains from automation allow healthcare professionals to focus more on direct patient care and less on paperwork, ultimately improving the quality of service.

However, the rise of AI in healthcare raises important ethical questions. As AI systems become more capable, concerns about data privacy, consent, and the potential for bias in AI algorithms must be addressed. Ensuring that AI is used responsibly and ethically will be essential for its continued success in the healthcare sector.

Analysis

This output strikes a balance between creativity and structure. It provides a comprehensive overview of AI in healthcare, covering various aspects like diagnostics, personalized medicine, and administrative tasks. The medium temperature setting ensures that the content is both creative and informative, making it well-suited for general articles, blog posts, or informational content where both creativity and clarity are important.

Comparison and Discussion

- **High Temperature (0.9):** This setting produces a more creative and engaging output, making it suitable for content that requires a conversational tone or emotional appeal. However, the output may lack the structured depth needed for formal or technical purposes.
- **Low Temperature (0.2):** The content generated is more structured, formal, and predictable. It's ideal for detailed reports or professional documentation where clarity and precision are paramount. The content is informative, with a focus on data and facts.
- **Very High Temperature (1.0):** This setting results in highly creative and abstract output, which can be engaging but lacks structure. It's suitable for brainstorming or generating highly imaginative content, but not ideal for detailed or factual writing.
- **Medium Temperature (0.5):** The output strikes a balance between creativity and structure, making it versatile for various content types. It's particularly useful for generating articles, blog posts, or reports where a mix of creativity and clarity is required.

By modifying characteristics like temperature and maximum tokens, users can create content that suits their unique requirements. While the high temperature encourages creativity for more interesting or abstract text, the low temperature is utilized to guarantee accuracy and clarity, which is appropriate for formal information. The medium setting is a sensible option for general-purpose content generation since it provides a versatile balance for a variety of content categories.

CONCLUSION

In order to effectively utilize GPT models across a range of applications and investigate advanced prompt engineering, the chapter highlights the Azure GPT Playground's exceptional flexibility and resilience. With an intuitive interface, the Playground streamlines the process of tailoring GPT model outputs to meet specific objectives, whether for crafting educational resources, streamlining customer service automation, or generating diverse forms of content. Its functionality is further enhanced by seamless integration into Azure's broader ecosystem, incorporating tools like Logic Apps and API services, which collectively underscore its value for developers and organizations alike. Nevertheless, the chapter underscores critical considerations, such as responsible usage, a thorough understanding of pricing structures, and adherence to industry regulations, to ensure that AI is deployed ethically. As artificial intelligence continues to advance, the Azure GPT Playground emerges as an indispensable resource, supporting the development of innovative, efficient, and ethically grounded AI solutions that hold the potential to revolutionize numerous sectors globally.

REFERENCES

[1] K.S. Kalyan, "A survey of GPT-3 family large language models including ChatGPT and GPT-4", *Natural Language Processing Journal,* vol. 6, p. 100048, 2024. [http://dx.doi.org/10.1016/j.nlp.2023.100048]

[2] M. Rosoł, J.S. Gąsior, J. Łaba, K. Korzeniewski, and M. Młyńczak, "Evaluation of the performance of GPT-3.5 and GPT-4 on the polish medical final examination", *Sci. Rep.,* vol. 13, no. 1, p. 20512, 2023. [http://dx.doi.org/10.1038/s41598-023-46995-z] [PMID: 37993519]

[3] R.A. Khan, M. Jawaid, A.R. Khan, and M. Sajjad, "ChatGPT - Reshaping medical education and clinical management", *Pak. J. Med. Sci.,* vol. 39, no. 2, pp. 605-607, 2023. [http://dx.doi.org/10.12669/pjms.39.2.7653] [PMID: 36950398]

[4] L. Zhang, J. Lin, Z. Kuang, S. Xu, and X. Hu, "SPL: A socratic playground for learning powered by large language model", Sep. 25, 2024. [http://dx.doi.org/10.48550/arXiv.2406.13919]

[5] A. Kabir, S. Shah, A. Haddad, and D.M.S. Raper, "Introducing our custom GPT: An example of the potential impact of personalized gpt builders on scientific writing", *World Neurosurg.,* vol. 193, pp. 461-468, 2025. [http://dx.doi.org/10.1016/j.wneu.2024.10.041] [PMID: 39442688]

SUBJECT INDEX

U

V

W

www.ingramcontent.com/pod-product-compliance
Lightning Source LLC
LaVergne TN
LVHW070952210926
848482LV00002B/189
9798898813628